MOST COMMON CHINESE CHARACTERS
- ORDERED BY FREQUENCY

的	de	possessive, adjectival suffix	是	shì	indeed, yes, right, to be, demonstrative pronoun	不	bù	no, not, un-, negative prefix
我	wǒ	our, us, i, me, my, we	一	yī	one, a, an, alone	有	yǒu	have, own, possess, exist
大	dà	big, great, vast, large, high	在	zài	be at, in, on, consist in, rest	人	rén	man, people, mankind, someone else
了	liǎo	to finish, particle of completed action	中	zhōng	central, center, middle, in the midst of	到	dào	go to, arrive, been to
资	zī	property, wealth, capital	要	yào	necessary, essential, necessity	可	kě	may, can, -able, possibly
以	yǐ	by means of, thereby, therefore, consider as	这	zhè	this, the, here	个	gè	numerary adjunct, piece, single
你	nǐ	you, second person pronoun	会	huì	to assemble, meet together, a meeting	好	hǎo	good, excellent, fine, well
为	wèi	do, handle, govern, act, be	上	shàng	top, superior, highest, go up, send up	来	lái	come, coming, return, returning
就	jiù	just, simply, to come, go to, to approach, near	学	xué	learning, knowledge, school	交	jiāo	mix, intersect, exchange, communicate, deliver
也	yě	classical final particle of strong affirmation	用	yòng	use, employ, apply, operate, use	能	néng	to be able, can, permitted to, ability
如	rú	if, supposing, as if, like, as	文	wén	literature, culture, writing	时	shí	time, season, era, age, period
没	méi	not, have not, none, to drown, sink	说	shuō	speak	他	tā	other, another, he, she, it
看	kàn	look, see, examine, scrutinize	提	tí	hold in hand, lift in hand	那	nà	that, that one, those
问	wèn	ask (about), inquire after	生	shēng	life, living, lifetime, birth	过	guò	pass, pass through, go across
下	xià	under, underneath, below, down, inferior	请	qǐng	ask, request, invite, please	天	tiān	sky, heaven, god, celestial
们	men	adjunct pronoun indicate plural	所	suǒ	place, location, numerary adjunct	多	duō	much, many, more than, over

麼	mó	dimi.	小	xiǎo	small, tiny, insignificant	想	xiǎng	think, speculate, plan, consider
得	dé	obtain, get, gain, acquire	之	zhī	it, him her, them, go to	还	huán	still, yet, also, besides
电	diàn	electricity, electric, lightning	出	chū	go out, send out, stand, produce	工	gōng	labor, work, worker, laborer
对	duì	correct, right, facing, opposed	都	dū	metropolis, capital, all, the whole, elegant	机	jī	machine, moment, chance
自	zì	self, private, personal, from	后	hòu	behind, rear, after, descendents	子	zǐ	offspring, child, fruit, seed of
而	ér	and, and then, and yet, but	讯	xùn	inquire, ask, examine, reproach	站	zhàn	stand up, a stand, station
去	qù	go away, leave, depart	心	xīn	heart, mind, intelligence, soul	只	zhī	single, one of pair, lone
知	zhī	know, perceive, comprehend	国	guó	nation, country, nation-state	台	tái	taiphoon
很	hěn	very, quite, much	信	xìn	trust, believe, letter	成	chéng	completed, finished, fixed
章	zhāng	composition, chapter, section	何	hé	what, why, where, which, how	同	tòng	alley, lane
道	dào	path, road, street, method, way	地	dì	earth, soil, ground, region	发	fǎ	hair
法	fǎ	law, rule, regulation, statute, France, French	无	wú	negative, no, not, lack, have no	然	rán	yes, certainly, pledge, promise
但	dàn	only, but, however, yet, still	吗	ma	final interrogative particle	当	dāng	bear, accept, undertake, just
于	yú	in, at, on, interjection alas!	本	běn	root, origin, source, basis	现	xiàn	appear, manifest, become visible
年	nián	year, new-years, person's age	前	qián	in front, forward, preceding	真	zhēn	real, actual, true, genuine
最	zuì	most, extremely, exceedingly	和	hé	harmony, peace, peaceful, calm	新	xīn	new, recent, fresh, modern

因	yīn	cause, reason, by, because (of)	果	guǒ	fruit, result	定	dìng	decide, settle, fix
意	yì	thought, idea, opinion, think	情	qíng	feeling, sentiment, emotion	点	diǎn	dot, speck, spot, point, degree
题	tí	forehead, title, headline, theme	其	qí	his, her, its, their, that	事	shì	affair, matter, business, to serve
方	fāng	a square, rectangle, a region, local	清	qīng	clear, pure, clean, peaceful	科	kē	section, department, science
样	yàng	shape, form, pattern, style	些	xiē	little, few, rather, somewhat	吧	ba	emphatic final particle
此	cǐ	this, these, in this case, then	位	wèi	throne, position, post, rank, status, seat	理	lǐ	reason, logic, manage
行	xíng	go, walk, move, travel, circulate	作	zuò	make, work, compose, write, act, perform	经	jīng	classic works, pass through
者	zhě	that which, he who, those who	什	shí	file of ten soldiers, mixed, miscellaneous	谢	xiè	thank, decline
名	míng	name, rank, title, position	日	rì	sun, day, daytime	正	zhèng	right, proper, correct
华	huá	flowery, illustrious, Chinese	话	huà	speech, talk, language, dialect	开	kāi	open, initiate, begin, start
实	shí	real, true, solid, honest	再	zài	again, twice, re-	城	chéng	castle, city, town, municipality
爱	ài	love, be fond of, like	与	yǔ	and, with, to, for, give, grant	二	èr	two, twice
动	dòng	move, happen, movement, action	比	bǐ	to compare, liken, comparison, than	高	gāo	high, tall, lofty, elevated
面	miàn	flour, dough, noodles	又	yòu	and, also, again, in addition	车	chē	cart, vehicle, carry in cart
力	lì	power, capability, influence	或	huò	or, either, else, perhaps, maybe	种	zhǒng	seed, race, offspring, to plant
像	xiàng	a picture, image, figure, to resemble	应	yìng	should, ought to, must	女	nǚ	woman, girl, feminine

教 jiào — teach, class	分 fēn — divide, small unit of time etc.	手 shǒu — hand
打 dǎ — strike, hit, beat, fight, attack	已 yǐ — already, finished, stop	次 cì — order, sequence, next
长 cháng — long, length, excel in, leader	太 tài — very, too, much, big, extreme	明 míng — bright, light, brilliant, clear
己 jǐ — self, oneself, personal, private	路 lù — road, path, street, journey	起 qǐ — rise, stand up, go up, begin
相 xiāng — mutual, reciprocal, each other	主 zhǔ — master, chief owner, host, lord	关 guān — frontier pass, close, relation
凤 fèng — male phoenix, symbol of joy	间 jiān — interval, space, place, between	呢 ní — interrogative or emphatic final, (Cant.) this
觉 jué — to wake up from sleep, conscious	该 gāi — should, ought to, need to	十 shí — pick up, accounting form of the numeral ten
外 wài — out, outside, external, foreign	凰 huáng — female phoenix	友 yǒu — friend, companion, fraternity
才 cái — talent, ability, just, only	民 mín — people, subjects, citizens	进 jìn — advance, make progress, enter
使 shǐ — , messenger, ambassador	她 tā — she, her	着 zhù — manifest, (Cant.) to wear
各 gè — each, individually, every, all	少 shǎo — few, less, inadequate	全 quán — maintain, keep whole or intact
两 liǎng — two, both, pair, couple, ounce	回 huí — return. turn around, a time	加 jiā — add to, increase, augment
将 jiāng — will, going to, future, general	感 gǎn — feel, perceive, emotion	第 dì — sequence, number, grade, degree
性 xìng — nature, character, sex	球 qiú — ball, sphere, globe, round	式 shì — style, system, formula, rule
把 bǎ — hold, take, guard, regard as	被 bèi — passive indicator 'by', bedding	老 lǎo — old, aged, experienced
公 gōng — fair, equitable, public, duke	龙 lóng — dragon, symbolic of emperor	程 chéng — journey, trip, schedule, agenda

论	lùn	debate, discuss, discourse
给	gěi	give, by, for
重	zhòng	heavy, weighty, double
校	xiào	school, military field officer
东	dōng	east, eastern, eastward
湾	wān	a bay, cove, inlet, bend of stream
解	jiě	loosen, unfasten, untie, explain
原	yuán	source, origin, beginning
先	xiān	first, former, previous
错	cuò	error, blunder, mistake, wrong
啊	a	exclamatory particle
乐	yuè	happy, glad, enjoyable, music
入	rù	enter, come in(to), join
较	jiào	compare, comparatively, more
由	yóu	cause, reason, from
快	kuài	rapid, quick, speedy, fast, soon
及	jí	extend, reach, come up to, and
听	tīng	hear, listen, understand, obey
体	tǐ	body, group, class, body, unit
里	lǐ	inside, interior, within
风	fēng	wind, air, manners, atmosphere
啦	la	final particle of assertion
等	děng	rank, grade, wait, equal, 'etc.'
月	yuè	moon, month, KangXi radical 74
管	guǎn	pipe, tube, duct, woodwind music
音	yīn	sound, tone, pitch, pronunciation
找	zhǎo	search, seek, look for, find
让	ràng	allow, permit, yield, concede
期	qí	period of time, date, time limit
四	sì	four
书	shū	book, letter, document, writings
从	cóng	from, by, since, whence, through
别	bié	separate, other, do not
水	shuǐ	water, liquid, lot5on, juice
做	zuò	work, make, act
常	cháng	common, normal, frequent, regular
您	nín	honorific for 'you'
见	jiàn	see, observe, behold, perceive
部	bù	part, division, section
美	měi	beautiful, pretty, pleasing
区	qū	area, district, region, ward, surname
否	fǒu	not, no, negative, final particle
网	wǎng	net, web, network
通	tōng	pass through, common, communicate
选	xuǎn	choose, select, elect, election
场	cháng	open space, field, market
它	tā	it, other
欢	huān	happy, pleased, glad, joy, to enjoy

数	shù	number, several, count, fate	表	biǎo	a watch, clock	怎	zěn	what? why? how?
至	zhì	reach, arrive, extremely, very	立	lì	stand, let stand, establish, set	内	nèi	inside, interior, domestic
合	hé	combine, unite, join, gather	目	mù	eye, look, see, division, topic	望	wàng	to look at, look forward, to hope, expect
认	rèn	recognize, know. understand	几	jǐ	how many? how much?, a few, some	社	shè	god of the soil and altars to him
告	gào	tell, announce, inform, accuse	更	gèng	more, still further, much more	版	bǎn	printing blocks, edition
度	dù	degree, system, manner, to consider	考	kǎo	examine, test, investigate	喜	xǐ	like, love, enjoy, joyful thing
头	tóu	head, top, chief, first, boss	难	nán	difficult, arduous, hard, unable	光	guāng	light, brilliant, shine, only
买	mǎi	buy, purchase, bribe, persuade	今	jīn	now, today, modern era	身	shēn	body, trunk, hull, rad. no. 158
许	xǔ	allow, permit, promise, betroth	弟	dì	young brother, junior, i, me	若	ruò	if, supposing, assuming, similar
算	suàn	count, calculate, figure, plan	记	jì	record, keep in mind, remember	代	dài	replace, generation
统	tǒng	govern, command, control, unite	处	chù	place, locale. department	完	wán	complete, finish, settle, whole
号	hào	mark, sign, symbol, number	接	jiē	receive, continue, catch, connect	言	yán	words, speech, speak, say
政	zhèng	government, political affairs	玩	wán	play with, joke, enjoy	师	shī	teacher, master, specialist, multitude, troops
字	zì	letter, character, word	并	bìng	combine, annex	男	nán	male, man, son, baron, surname
计	jì	plan, plot, stratagem, scheme	谁	shuí	who? whom? whose? anyone?	山	shān	mountain, hill, peak
张	zhāng	stretch, extend, expand, sheet	党	dǎng	political party, gang, faction	每	měi	every, each

且	qiě	moreover, also (post-subject), about to	结	jié	knot, tie, join, connect	改	gǎi	change, alter, improve, remodel
非	fēi	not, negative, non-, oppose	星	xīng	a star, planet, any point of light	连	lián	join, connect, continuous, even
哈	hā	sound of laughter	建	jiàn	build, establish, erect, found	放	fàng	put, release, free, liberate
直	zhí	straight, erect, vertical	转	zhuǎn	shift, move, turn	报	bào	report, tell, announce
活	huó	live, exist, survive, lively	设	shè	build, establish, display, particle of hypothesis	变	biàn	change, transform, alter, rebel
指	zhǐ	finger, toe, point, indicate	气	qì	air, gas, steam, vapor, spirit	研	yán	grind, rub, study, research
陈	chén	exhibit, display, plead, surname	试	shì	test, try, experiment	西	xī	west(ern), westward, occident
五	wǔ	five, surname	希	xī	rare, hope, expect, strive for	取	qū	take, receive, obtain, select
神	shén	spirit, god, supernatural being	化	huà	change, convert, reform, -ize	物	wù	thing, substance, creature
王	wáng	king, ruler, royal, surname	战	zhàn	war, fighting, battle	近	jìn	near, close, approach, intimate
世	shì	generation, world, era	受	shòu	receive, accept, get, bear, stand	义	yì	right conduct, righteousness
反	fǎn	reverse, opposite, contrary, anti	单	dān	single, individual, only, lone	死	sǐ	die, dead, death
任	rèn	trust to, rely on, appoint, to bear, duty	跟	gēn	heel, to follow, accompany, with	便	biàn	convenience, ease, expedient
空	kōng	empty, hollow, bare, deserted	林	lín	forest, grove, surname	士	shì	scholar, gentleman, soldier
台	tái	taiphoon	却	què	still, but, decline, retreat	北	běi	north, northern, northward
队	duì	team, group, army unit	功	gōng	achievement, merit, good result	必	bì	surely, most certainly, must

声 shēng sound, voice, noise, tone, music	写 xiě write, draw, sketch, compose	平 píng flat, level, even, peaceful
影 yǐng shadow, image, reflection, photograph	业 yè profession, business, trade	金 jīn gold, metals in general, money
档 dǎng shelf, frame, crosspiece	片 piàn slice, splinter, strip, rad. 91	讨 tǎo to discuss, ask for, beg, demand, dun, marry
色 sè color, tint, hue, shade, form, body, beauty	容 róng looks, appearance, figure, form	央 yāng center, conclude, run out, beg
妳 nǎi you (f.)	向 xiàng once upon time, period of time	市 shì market, fair, city, town, trade
则 zé rule, law, regulation, grades	员 yuán member, personnel, staff member	兴 xīng thrive, prosper, flourish
利 lì gains, advantage, profit, merit	强 qiáng strong, powerful, energetic	白 bái white, pure, unblemished, bright
价 jià price, value	安 ān peaceful, tranquil, quiet	呵 hē scold, laughing sound, yawn
特 tè special, unique, distinguished	思 sī think, consider, ponder, final particle	叫 jiào cry, shout, hail, greet, call
总 zǒng collect, overall, altogether	办 bàn manage, do, handle, deal with	保 bǎo protect, safeguard, defend, care
花 huā flower, blossoms	议 yì consult, talk over, discuss	传 chuán summon, propagate, transmit
元 yuán first, dollar, origin, head	求 qiú seek, demand, request, beseech	份 fèn portion, part, duty
件 jiàn numerary adjunct for article, matter	持 chí sustain, support, hold, grasp	万 wàn ten thousand, innumerable
未 wèi not yet, 8th terrestrial branch	究 jiù examine, investigate	决 jué decide, determine, judge
投 tóu throw, cast, fling, pitch, jump	哪 nǎ which? where? how?	喔 wō descriptive of crying or of crowing
笑 xiào smile, laugh, giggle, snicker	猫 māo cat	组 zǔ class, section, department

独	dú	alone, single, solitary, only
级	jí	level, rank, class, grade
走	zǒu	walk, go on foot, run, leave
支	zhī	disperse, pay, support, branch
曾	céng	already, sign of past
标	biāo	a mark, symbol, label, sign, standard
流	liú	flow, circulate, drift, class
竹	zhú	bamboo, flute, KangXi radical 118
兄	xiōng	elder brother
阿	ā	prefix for people's names, used in transliteration
室	shì	room, home, house, chamber
卡	qiǎ	card, punch card, calorie
马	mǎ	horse, surname, KangXi radical 187
共	gòng	together with, all, total, to share
需	xū	need, require, must
海	hǎi	sea, ocean, maritime
口	kǒu	mouth, open end, entrance, gate
门	mén	gate, door, entrance, opening
般	bān	sort, manner, kind, category
线	xiàn	thread, line, wire, clue
语	yǔ	language, words, saying, expression
命	mìng	life, destiny, fate, luck, an order, instruction
观	guān	see, observe, view, appearance
视	shì	look at, inspect, observe, see
朋	péng	friend, pal, acquaintance
联	lián	connect, join, associate, ally
参	cān	take part in, intervene, ginseng
格	gé	pattern, standard, form, style
黄	huáng	yellow, surname
钱	qián	money, currency, coins
修	xiū	study, repair, cultivate
失	shī	lose, make mistake, neglect
儿	ér	son, child, oneself, final part
住	zhù	reside, live at, dwell, lodge, stop
八	bā	eight, all around, all sides
脑	nǎo	brain
板	bǎn	boss, the owner, person in charge
吃	chī	eat, drink, suffer, endure, bear
另	lìng	another, separate, other
换	huàn	change, exchange, substitute
即	jí	promptly, quickly, immediately
象	xiàng	elephant, ivory, figure, image
料	liào	consider, conjecture, materials, ingredients
录	lù	copy
拿	ná	take, hold, grasp, bring, with
专	zhuān	monopolize, take sole possession
远	yuǎn	distant, remote, far, profound
速	sù	quick, prompt, speedy

基 jī foundation, base	帮 bāng to help, assist, to defend, shoe upper	形 xíng form, shape, appearance
确 què sure, certain, real, true	候 hòu wait, expect, visit, greet	装 zhuāng dress, clothes, decorate, fill
孩 hái baby, child, children	备 bèi prepare, ready, perfect	歌 gē song, lyrics, sing, chant, praise
界 jiè boundary, limit, domain, society, the world	除 chú eliminate, remove, except	南 nán south, southern part, southward
器 qì receptacle, vessel, instrument	画 huà painting	诉 sù accuse, sue, inform, narrate
差 chāi to differ, different, wrong, nearly, almost	讲 jiǎng explain, discuss, talk	类 lèi class, group, kind, category
英 yīng petal, flower, leaf, brave, a hero	案 àn table, bench, legal case	带 dài belt, girdle, band, strap, zone
久 jiǔ long time (ago), time passage, grow late	乎 hū interrogative or exclamatory final particle	掉 diào turn, move, shake, wag, drop down
迷 mí bewitch, charm, infatuate	量 liàng measure, quantity, capacity	引 yǐn to pull, draw out, attract, to stretch
整 zhěng orderly, neat, tidy, whole	似 sì resemble, similar to, as if, seem	耶 yé used in transliteration
奇 qí strange, unusual, uncanny, occult	制 zhì make, manufacture, produce	边 biān edge, margin, side, border
型 xíng pattern, model, type, law, mold	超 chāo jump over, leap over, surpass	识 shì recognize, understand, know
虽 suī although, even if	怪 guài strange, unusual, peculiar	飞 fēi fly, go quickly, dart, high
始 shǐ begin, start, then, only then	品 pǐn article, product, commodity	运 yùn luck, fortune, ship, transport
赛 sài compete, contend, contest, race	费 fèi expenses, expenditures, fee	梦 mèng dream, visionary, wishful
故 gù ancient, old, reason, because	班 bān class, group, grade, squad, job	权 quán power, right, authority

破 pò	验 yàn	眼 yǎn
break, ruin, destroy, rout	test, examine, inspect, verify	eye, eyelet, hole, opening
满 mǎn	念 niàn	造 zào
fill, full, satisfied	think of, recall, study	construct, build, make, begin, prepare
军 jūn	精 jīng	务 wù
army, military, soldiers, troops	essence, semen, spirit	affairs, business, must, should
留 liú	服 fú	六 liù
stop, halt, stay, detain, keep	clothes, wear, dress	number six
图 tú	收 shōu	舍 shě
diagram, chart, map, picture	gather together, collect, harvest	discard, give up willingly, give alms
半 bàn	读 dú	愿 yuàn
half	read, study, pronounce	desire, want, wish, ambition
李 lǐ	底 dǐ	约 yuē
plum, judge, surname	bottom, underneath, underside	treaty, agreement, covenant
雄 xióng	课 kè	答 dá
male of species, hero, manly	lesson, course, classwork	answer, reply, return, assent to
令 lìng	深 shēn	票 piào
command, order, 'commandant', magistrate	deep, depth, far, very, extreme	slip of paper or bamboo, ticket
达 dá	演 yǎn	早 zǎo
arrive at, reach, intelligent	perform, put on, exercise	early, soon, morning
卖 mài	棒 bàng	够 gòu
sell, betray, show off	stick, club, truncheon, hit	enough, adequate
黑 hēi	院 yuàn	假 jiǎ
black, dark, evil, sinister	courtyard, yard, court, school	falsehood, deception, vacation
曲 qǔ	火 huǒ	准 zhǔn
crooked, bent, wrong, false	fire, flame, burn, anger, rage	rule, guideline, standard
百 bǎi	谈 tán	胜 shèng
one hundred, numerous, many	talk, conversation, surname	victory, excel, be better than
碟 dié	术 shù	推 tuī
small dish, plate	art, skill, special feat, method, technique	push, expel, push forward
存 cún	治 zhì	离 lí
exist, live, be, survive, remain	govern, regulate, administer	leave, depart, go away, separate

易	yì — change, easy	往	wǎng — go, depart, past, formerly	况	kuàng — condition, situation, furthermore
晚	wǎn — night, evening, late	示	shì — show, manifest, demonstrate	证	zhèng — proof, evidence, testify, verify
段	duàn — section, piece, division	导	dǎo — direct, guide, lead, conduct	伤	shāng — wound, injury, fall ill from
调	diào — transfer, move, change, tune	团	tuán — sphere, ball, circle, mass, lump	七	qī — seven
永	yǒng — long, perpetual, eternal, forever	刚	gāng — hard, tough, rigid, strong	哥	gē — elder brother
甚	shén — great extent, considerably	德	dé — ethics, morality, virtue	杀	shā — kill, slaughter, murder, hurt, to pare off
怕	pà — to fear, be afraid of, apprehensive	包	bāo — wrap, pack, bundle, package	列	liè — a line, to arrange in order, classify
概	gài — generally, approximately	照	zhào — shine, illumine, reflect	夜	yè — night, dark, in night, by night
排	pái — row, rank, line	客	kè — guest, traveller, customer	绝	jué — cut
软	ruǎn — soft, flexible, pliable, weak	商	shāng — commerce, business, trade	根	gēn — root, base(d on), foundation
九	jiǔ — nine	切	qiē — cut, mince, slice, carve	条	tiáo — clause, condition, string, stripe
集	jí — assemble, collect together	千	qiān — thousand, many, numerous, very	落	luò — fall, drop, net income, surplus
竟	jìng — finally, after all, at last	越	yuè — exceed, go beyond, the more …	待	dài — treat, entertain, receive, wait
忘	wàng — forget, neglect, miss, omit	尽	jìn — exhaust, use up, deplete	据	jù — to occupy, take possession of, a base
双	shuāng — set of two, pair, couple, both	供	gōng — supply, provide for, offer in worship	称	chēng — call, name, brand, address, say
座	zuò — seat, stand, base	值	zhí — price	消	xiāo — vanish, die out, melt away

产	chǎn	give birth	红	hóng	red, vermillion, blush, flush	跑	pǎo	run, flee, leave in hurry
嘛	ma	final exclamatory particle	园	yuán	garden, park, orchard	附	fù	adhere to, append, rely on near to
硬	yìng	hard, firm, strong, obstinate	云	yún	clouds, Yunnan province	游	yóu	to swim, float, drift, wander, roam
展	zhǎn	open, unfold, stretch, extend	执	zhí	hold in hand, keep, carry out	闻	wén	hear, smell, make known, news
唱	chàng	sing, chant, call, ditty, song	育	yù	produce, give birth to, educate	斯	sī	this, thus, such, to lop off, emphatic particle
某	mǒu	certain thing or person	技	jì	skill, ability, talent, ingenuity	唉	āi	alas, exclamation of surprise or pain
息	xī	rest, put stop to, end, cease	苦	kǔ	bitter, hardship, suffering	质	zhí	matter, material, substance
油	yóu	oil, fat, grease, lard, paints	救	jiù	save, rescue, relieve, help, aid	效	xiào	result, effect, effectiveness
须	xū	beard, whiskers, whisker-like	介	jiè	forerunner, herald, harbinger, to lie between	首	shǒu	head, first, leader, chief, a poem
助	zhù	help, aid, assist	职	zhí	duty, profession, office, post	例	lì	precedent, example, regulation
热	rè	hot, heat, fever, restless, zeal	毕	bì	end, finish, conclude, completed	节	jié	knot, node, joint, section
害	hài	injure, harm, destroy, kill	击	jí	strike, hit, beat, attack, fight	乱	luàn	confusion, state of chaos, create chaos, revolt
态	tài	manner, bearing, attitude	嗯	ēn	(a groaning sound)	宝	bǎo	treasure, jewel, precious, rare
倒	dǎo	fall over, lie down, take turns	注	zhù	explain, annotate, make entry	停	tíng	stop, suspend, delay, suitable
古	gǔ	old, classic, ancient	输	shū	transport, carry, haul	规	guī	rules, regulations, customs, law
福	fú	happiness, good fortune, blessing	亲	qīn	relatives, parents, intimate	查	chá	investigate, examine, seek into

复	fù	cover, tip over, return, reply	步	bù	step, pace, walk, stroll	举	jǔ	raise, lift up, recommend
鱼	yú	fish, surname, KangXi radical 195	断	duàn	sever, cut off, interrupt	终	zhōng	end, finally, in the end
轻	qīng	light, easy, simple, gentle	环	huán	jade ring or bracelet, ring	练	liàn	practice, drill, exercise, train
印	yìn	print, seal, stamp, chop, mark	随	suí	follow, listen to, submit, to accompany	依	yī	rely on, be set in, consent, obey a wish
趣	qù	what attracts one's attention	限	xiàn	boundary, limit, line	响	xiǎng	make sound, make noise, sound
省	shěng	province, save, economize	局	jú	bureau, office, circumstance	续	xù	continue, carry on, succeed
司	sī	take charge of, control, manage, officer	角	jiǎo	horn, angle, corner, point	简	jiǎn	simple, terse, succinct, letter
极	jí	extreme, utmost, furthest, final	干	gàn	trunk of tree or of human body	篇	piān	chapter, section, essay, article
罗	luó	net for catching birds, gauze	佛	fó	Buddha, of Buddhism, merciful percon	克	kè	subdue, overcome, cut down
阳	yáng	male' principle, light, sun	武	wǔ	military, martial, warlike	疑	yí	doubt, question, suspect
送	sòng	see off, send off, dispatch, give	拉	lā	pull, drag, seize, hold, lengthen	习	xí	practice, flapping wings
源	yuán	spring, source, head, surname	免	miǎn	spare, excuse from, evade	志	zhì	write down, record, magazine
鸟	niǎo	bird, KangXi radical 196	烦	fán	bother, vex, trouble, troublesome	足	zú	foot, attain, satisfy, enough
馆	guǎn	public building	仍	réng	yet, still, as ever, again, keep-ing, continuing	低	dī	low, to lower, hang, bend, bow
广	guǎng	broad, wide, extensive	土	tǔ	soil, earth, items made of earth	呀	yā	particle used to express surprise
楼	lóu	building of two or more stories	坏	huài	bad, spoil(ed), ruin, destroy	兵	bīng	soldier, troops

显	xiǎn — manifest, display, evident, clear	率	lǜ — to lead, ratio, rate, limit	圣	shèng — holy, sacred, sage
码	mǎ — number, numerals, yard, symbol	众	zhòng — multitude, crowd, masses, public	争	zhēng — to dispute, fight, contend, strive
初	chū — beginning, initial, primary	误	wù — err, make mistake, interfere	楚	chǔ — name of feudal state, clear
责	zé — one's responsibility, duty	境	jìng — boundary, frontier, area, region	野	yě — open country, field, wilderness
预	yù — prepare, arrange, in advance	具	jù — tool, implement, draw up, write	智	zhì — wisdom, knowledge, intelligence
压	yā — press, oppress, crush, pressure	系	xì — attach, connect, unite, fasten	青	qīng — blue, green, black, young
贵	guì — expensive, costly, valuable	顺	shùn — obey, submit to, go along with	负	fù — load, burden, carry, bear
魔	mó — demon, evil spirits, magic power	适	shì — match, comfortable, just	哇	wā — vomit, cry of an infant
测	cè — measure, estimate, conjecture	慢	màn — slow(ly), leisurely, sluggish	怀	huái — bosom, breast, carry in bosom
懂	dǒng — understand, comprehend	史	shǐ — history, chronicle, annals	配	pèi — match, pair, equal, blend
呜	wū — sound of crying, sobbing	味	wèi — taste, smell, odor, delicacy	亦	yì — also, too, likewise
医	yī — cure, heal, doctor, medical	迎	yíng — receive, welcome, greet	舞	wǔ — dance, posture, prance, brandish
恋	liàn — love, long for, yearn for, love	细	xì — fine, tiny, slender, thin	灌	guàn — pour, water, irrigate, flood
甲	jiǎ — armor, shell, fingernails	帝	dì — supreme ruler, emperor, god	句	jù — sentence
属	shǔ — class, category, type, to belong to	灵	líng — spirit, soul, spiritual world	评	píng — appraise, criticize, evaluate
骑	qí — ride horseback, mount, cavalry	宜	yí — suitable, right, fitting, proper	败	bài — be defeated, decline, fail

左	zuǒ	left, east, unorthodox, improper	追	zhuī	pursue, chase after, expel	狂	kuáng	insane, mad, violent, wild
敢	gǎn	to dare, venture, bold, brave	春	chūn	spring, wanton	狗	gǒu	dog, canis familiaris
际	jì	border, boundary, juncture	遇	yù	meet, come across, encounter	族	zú	a family clan, ethnic group, tribe
群	qún	group, crowd, multitude, mob	痛	tòng	pain, ache, sorry, sad, bitter	右	yòu	right, west, right-wing
康	kāng	peaceful, quiet, happy, healthy	佳	jia	good, auspicious, beautiful, delightful	杨	yáng	willow, poplar, aspen, surname
木	mù	tree, wood, lumber, wooden	病	bìng	illness, sickness, disease	戏	xì	theatrical play, show
项	xiàng	neck, nape of neck, sum, funds	抓	zhuā	scratch, clutch, seize, grab	征	zhēng	summon, recruit, musical note
善	shàn	good, virtuous, charitable, kind	官	guān	official, public servant	护	hù	protect, guard, defend, shelter
博	bó	gamble, play games, wide, broad	补	bǔ	mend, patch, fix, repair, restore	石	shí	stone, rock, mineral, rad. 112
尔	ěr	you, that, those, final particle	营	yíng	encampment, barracks, manage	历	lì	take place, past, history
只	zhī	single, one of pair, lone	按	àn	put hand on, press down with hand	妹	mèi	younger sister
里	lǐ	inside, interior, within	编	biān	knit, weave, arrange, compile	岁	suì	year, age, harvest
择	zé	select, choose, pick out	温	wēn	lukewarm, warm, tepid, mild	守	shǒu	defend, protect, guard, conserve
血	xiě	blood, radical number 143	领	lǐng	neck, collar, lead, guide	寻	xún	seek, search, look for, ancient
田	tián	field, arable land, cultivated	养	yǎng	raise, rear, bring up, support	谓	wèi	say, tell, call, name, be called
居	jū	live, dwell, reside, sit	异	yì	different, unusual, strange	雨	yǔ	rain, rainy, KangXi radical 173

止	zhǐ	stop, halt, desist, detain
烂	làn	rotten, spoiled, decayed
拜	bài	do obeisance, bow, kowtow
浪	làng	wave, wasteful, reckless
急	jí	quick, quickly, urgent, pressing
激	jī	arouse, excite, incite, quickly
忙	máng	busy, pressed for time, hustling
牛	niú	cow, ox, bull, KangXi radical93
维	wéi	maintain, preserve, safeguard
抱	bào	embrace, hold in arms, enfold
词	cí	words, phrase, expression
签	qiān	sign, endorse, slip of paper
幕	mù	curtain, screen, tent
爽	shuǎng	happy, cheerful, refreshing
吴	wú	one of warring states, surname
致	zhì	delicate, fine, dense
跳	tiào	jump, leap, vault, bounce, dance
优	yōu	superior, excellent, actor
恶	è	evil, wicked, bad, foul
核	hé	seed, kernel, core, nut, atom
状	zhuàng	form, appearance, shape, official
模	mó	model, standard, pattern, copy
良	liáng	good, virtuous, respectable
垒	lěi	rampart, military wall
静	jìng	quiet, still, motionless, gentle
势	shì	power, force, tendency
亚	yà	Asia, second, used as a prefix to names
悲	bēi	sorrow, grief, sorry, sad
毒	dú	poison, venom, poisonous
缘	yuán	hem, margin, reason, cause, karma, fate
兰	lán	orchid, elegant, graceful
江	jiāng	large river, yangzi, surname
君	jūn	sovereign, monarch, ruler, chief, prince
封	fēng	letter, envelope, feudal
啥	shà	what?
聊	liáo	somewhat, slightly, at least
陆	lù	land, continental, army
攻	gōng	attack, assault, criticize
剧	jù	theatrical plays, opera, drama
增	zēng	increase, add to, augment
阵	zhèn	column, row or file of troops
严	yán	strict, rigorous, rigid, stern
夫	fū	man, male adult, husband, those
密	mì	dense, thick, close, intimate
厂	chǎng	factory, plant, workshop, mill
店	diàn	shop, store, inn, hotel
睡	shuì	sleep, doze
宿	sù	stop, rest, lodge, stay overnight, constellation

翻	fān	flip over, upset, capsize	香	xiāng	fragrant, sweet smelling, incense	蛮	mán	barbarians, barbarous, savage
警	jǐng	guard, watch, alert, alarm	控	kòng	accuse, charge, control	赵	zhào	surname, ancient state
冷	lěng	cold, cool, lonely	威	wēi	pomp, power, powerful, dominate	微	wēi	small, prefix micro-, trifling
坐	zuò	sit, seat, ride, travel by	周	zhōu	Zhou dynasty, circumference	宗	zōng	lineage, ancestry, ancestor, clan
普	pǔ	universal, general, widespread	登	dēng	rise, mount, board, climb	母	mǔ	mother, female elders, female
络	luò	enmesh, wrap around, web, net	午	wǔ	noon, 7th terrestrial branch	恐	kǒng	fear, fearful, apprehensive
套	tào	case, cover, wrapper, envelope	巴	bā	greatly desire, anxiously hope	杂	zá	mixed, blended, mix, mingle
创	chuàng	establish, create, knife cut	旧	jiù	old, ancient, former, past	辑	jí	gather up, collect, edit, compile
幸	xìng	luck(ily), favor, fortunately	剑	jiàn	sword, dagger, saber	亮	liàng	bright, brilliant, radiant, light
述	shù	narrate, state, express	堂	táng	hall, government office	酒	jiǔ	wine, spirits, liquor, alcoholic beverage
丽	lì	beautiful, magnificent, elegant	牌	pái	signboard, placard	仔	zǐ	small thing, child, young animal
脚	jiǎo	foot, base, leg, foundation	突	tú	suddenly, abruptly, unexpectedly	搞	gǎo	to clear, clarify
父	fù	father, KangXi radical 88	俊	jùn	talented, capable, handsome	暴	bào	violent, brutal, tyrannical
防	fáng	defend, prevent, embankment	吉	jí	lucky, propitious, good	礼	lǐ	social custom, manners, courtesy, rites
素	sù	white (silk), plain, vegetarian, formerly	招	zhāo	beckon, summon, recruit, levy	草	cǎo	grass, straw, thatch, herbs
周	zhōu	Zhou dynasty, circumference	房	fáng	house, building, room	餐	cān	eat, dine, meal, food

虑	lǜ	be concerned, worry about
充	chōng	fill, be full, supply
府	fǔ	prefecture, prefect, government
背	bèi	back, back side, behind, betray
典	diǎn	law, canon, documentation, classic, scripture
仁	rén	humaneness, benevolence, kindness
漫	màn	overflow of water, spreading
景	jǐng	scenery, view, conditions
绍	shào	continue, carry on, hand down, to join
诸	zhū	several, various
琴	qín	Chinese lute or guitar
忆	yì	remember, reflect upon, memory
援	yuán	aid, assist, lead, cite
尤	yóu	especially, particularly
缺	quē	be short of, lack, gap, deficit
扁	biǎn	flat, tablet, signboard
骂	mà	accuse, blame, curse, scold
纯	chún	pure, clean, simple
惜	xī	pity, regret, rue, begrudge
授	shòu	give to, transmit, confer
皮	pí	skin, hide, fur, feather, outer
松	sōng	lax, loose, loosen, relax
委	wěi	appoint, send, commission
湖	hú	a lake, Hubei, Hunan, bluish-green
诚	chéng	sincere, honest, true, real
麻	má	hemp, jute, flax, sesame
置	zhì	place, lay out, set aside
靠	kào	lean on, trust, depend on, near
继	jì	continue, maintain, carry on
判	pàn	judge, discriminate, conclude
益	yì	profit, benefit, advantage
波	bō	waves, breakers, undulations
姐	jiě	elder sister, young lady
既	jì	already, de facto, since, then
射	shè	shoot, eject, issue forth, emit
欲	yù	desire, want, long for, intend
刻	kè	carve, engrave, quarter hour
堆	duī	heap, pile, crowd, pile up
释	shì	interprete, elucidate, release
含	hán	hold in mouth, cherish, contain
承	chéng	inherit, receive, succeed
退	tuì	step back, retreat, withdraw
莫	mò	do not, is not, can not, negative
刘	liú	surname, kill, destroy
昨	zuó	yesterday, in former times, past
旁	páng	side, by side, close by, near
纪	jì	record, annal, historical account
赶	gǎn	pursue, follow, expel, drive away

制	zhì	make, manufacture, produce	尚	shàng	still, yet, even, fairly, rather	艺	yì	art, talent, ability, craft
肉	ròu	flesh, meat, KangXi radical 130	律	lǜ	statute, principle, regulation	铁	tiě	iron, strong, solid, firm
奏	zòu	memorialize emperor, report	树	shù	tree, plant, set up, establish	毛	máo	hair, fur, feathers, coarse
罪	zuì	crime, sin, vice, evil, hardship	笔	bǐ	writing brush, write, stroke	彩	cǎi	hue, color, variegated colors
归	guī	return, return to, revert to	弹	dàn	pellet, bullet, shot, shell	虎	hǔ	tiger, brave, fierce, surname
卫	wèi	guard, protect, defend	刀	dāo	knife, old coin, measure	皆	jiē	all, every, everybody
键	jiàn	door bolt, lock bolt, key	售	shòu	sell	块	kuài	piece, lump, dollar
险	xiǎn	narrow pass, strategic point, dangerous	荣	róng	glory, honor, flourish, prosper	播	bò	sow, spread, broadcast, case away, reject
施	shī	grant, bestow, give, act, name	铭	míng	inscribe, engrave, unforgettably	汉	hàn	the Chinese people, Chinese language
赏	shǎng	reward, grant, bestow, appreciate	欣	xīn	happy, joyous, delighted	升	shēng	arise, go up, hoist, advance
叶	xié	leaf, petal, page of book, period	萤	yíng	glow-worm, luminous insect	载	zài	load, carry, transport, convey
嘿	mò	be silent, be quiet	弄	nòng	do, play or fiddle with, alley	钟	zhōng	clock, bell
付	fù	give, deliver, pay, hand over, entrust	寄	jì	send, transmit, mail, rely on	鬼	guǐ	ghost, spirit of dead, devil
哦	é	oh? really? is that so?	灯	dēng	lantern, lamp	呆	ái	dull, dull-minded, simple, stupid
洋	yáng	ocean, sea, foreign, western	嘻	xī	mirthful, happy, interjection	布	bù	cotton cloth, textiles, linen
磁	cí	magnetic, magnetism, porcelain	荐	jiàn	offer, present, recommend	检	jiǎn	check, examine

派	pài	school of thought, sect, branch	构	gòu	frame, building, structure	妈	mā	mother, mama
蓝	lán	blue, indigo plant, surname	贴	tiē	paste to, stick on, attached to	猪	zhū	pig, hog
策	cè	scheme, plan, to whip, urge	纸	zhǐ	paper	暗	àn	dark, obscure, in secret, covert
巧	qiǎo	skillful, ingenious, clever	努	nǔ	to exert, strive, make an effort, to pout	雷	léi	thunder
架	jià	rack, stand, prop, prop up	享	xiǎng	enjoy	宣	xuān	declare, announce, proclaim
逢	féng	come upon, happen meet, flatter	均	jūn	equal, even, fair, all, also	担	dān	carry, bear, undertake
启	qǐ	open, begin	济	jì	to help, aid, relieve, to ferry, cross	罢	bà	cease, finish, stop, give up
呼	hū	breathe sigh, exhale, call, shout	划	huà	delineate, painting, picture, drawing, draw	伟	wěi	great, robust, extraordinary
岛	dǎo	island	歉	qiàn	deficient, lacking, insufficient	郭	guō	outer part (of a city), surname
训	xùn	teach, instruct, exegesis	穿	chuān	penetrate, pierce, drill, wear	详	xiáng	detailed, complete, thorough
沙	shā	sand, gravel, pebbles, granulated	督	dū	supervise, oversee, direct	梅	méi	plums, prunes, surname
顾	gù	look back, look at, look after	敌	dí	enemy, foe, rival, resist	协	xié	be united, cooperate
轮	lún	wheel, revolve, turn, recur	略	lvè	approximately, roughly, outline	慧	huì	bright, intelligent, intelligence
幻	huàn	illusion, fantasy, mirage	脸	liǎn	face, cheek, reputation	短	duǎn	short, brief, deficient, lacking
鹰	yīng	eagle, falcon, Accipiter species (various)	冲	chōng	rush against, charge ahead	朝	zhāo	dynasty, morning
忍	rěn	endure, bear, suffer, forbear	游	yóu	to swim, float, drift, wander, roam	河	hé	river, stream, yellow river

批 pī — comment, criticize, wholesale	混 hǔn — to mix, blend, mingle, to bumble along	窗 chuāng — window
乡 xiāng — country, rural, village	蛋 dàn — eggs, term of abuse	季 jì — quarter of year, season, surname
散 sàn — scatter, disperse, break up	册 cè — book, volume	弃 qì — reject, abandon, discard
熟 shóu — well-cooked, ripe, familiar with	奖 jiǎng — prize, reward, give award to	唯 wéi — only, yes
藏 cáng — hide, conceal, hoard, store up	婚 hūn — get married, marriage, wedding	镜 jìng — mirror, lens, glass, glasses
紧 jǐn — tense, tight, taut, firm, secure	猜 cāi — guess, conjecture, suppose, feel	喝 hē — drink, shout, call out
尊 zūn — respect, revere, venerate, honor	干 gān — dry, first hexagram, warming principle of the sun	县 xiàn — county, district, subdivision
伯 bó — older brother, father's elder brother	偏 piān — inclined one side, slanting	偷 tōu — to steal, burglar, thief
秋 qiū — autumn, fall, year	层 céng — storey, layer, floor, stratum	颗 kē — grain, kernel
食 shí — eat, meal, food, KangXi radical number 184	淡 dàn — weak, watery, insipid, tasteless	申 shēn — to state to a superior, report, extend
冠 guān — cap, crown, headgear	衣 yī — clothes, clothing, cover, skin	仅 jǐn — only, merely, solely, just
帐 zhàng — tent, screen, mosquito net	赞 zàn — help, support, assist, aid	购 gòu — buy, purchase, hire
犯 fàn — commit crime, violate, criminal	敬 jìng — respect, honor, respectfully	勇 yǒng — brave, courageous, fierce
洲 zhōu — continent, island, islet	束 shù — bind, control, restrain, bale	斗 dòu — struggle, fight, compete, contend
徒 tú — disciple, follower, go on foot	嘉 jiā — excellent, joyful, auspicious	柔 róu — soft, gentle, pliant
绩 jī — spin, achievements	笨 bèn — foolish, stupid, dull, awkward	拥 yǒng — embrace, hug, squeeze, crowd

漂	piāo	float, drift, tossed about	狮	shī	lion	诗	shī	poetry, poem, verse, ode
围	wéi	surround, encircle, corral	乖	guāi	rebel, crafty, shrewd	孤	gū	orphan, fatherless, solitary
姓	xìng	one's family name, clan, people	吸	xī	inhale, suck in, absorb, attract	私	sī	private, personal, secret
避	bì	avoid, turn aside, escape, hide	范	fàn	pattern, model, rule, law	抗	kàng	resist, oppose, defy, reject
盖	gài	cover, hide, protect	祝	zhù	pray for happiness or blessings	序	xù	series, serial order, sequence
晓	xiǎo	dawn, daybreak, clear, explicit	富	fù	abundant, ample, rich, wealthy	译	yì	translate, decode, encode
巨	jù	large, great, enormous, chief	秀	xiù	ear of grain, flowering, luxuriant, refined	馀	yú	remainder
辉	huī	brightness, luster, brilliance	插	chā	insert, stick into, plant	察	chá	examine, investigate, notice
庆	qìng	congratulate, celebrate	积	jī	accumulate, store up, amass	愈	yù	more and more, even more
端	duān	end, extreme, head, beginning	移	yí	change place, shift, move about	宫	gōng	palace, temple, dwelling, enclose
挥	huī	direct, wipe away, squander	爆	bào	crackle, pop, burst, explode	港	gǎng	port, harbor, small stream, bay
雪	xuě	snow, wipe away shame, avenge	硕	shuò	great, eminent, large, big	借	jiè	borrow, lend, make pretext of
帅	shuài	commander, commander-in-chief	丢	diū	discard, reject, lose	括	guā	include, embrace, enclose
挂	guà	hang, suspend, suspense	盘	pán	tray, plate, dish, examine	偶	ǒu	accidentally, coincidently, an idol
末	mò	final, last, end, insignificant	厅	tīng	hall, central room	朱	zhū	cinnabar, vermilion, surname
凡	fán	all, any, every, ordinary, common	惊	jīng	frighten, surprise, startle	货	huò	goods, commodities, products

灭	miè extinguish, wipe out, exterminate	醒	xǐng wake up, sober up, startle	虚	xū false, worthless, empty, hollow
瑞	ruì felicitous omen, auspicious	拍	pāi clap, tap, beat, beat or rhythm	遗	yí lose, articles lost, omit
忠	zhōng loyalty, devotion, fidelity	志	zhì write down, record, magazine	透	tòu penetrate, pass through
烈	liè fiery, violent, vehement, ardent	银	yín silver, cash, money, wealth	顶	dǐng top, peak, carry on head, very
雅	yǎ elegant, graceful, refined	诺	nuò promise, assent, approve	圆	yuán circle, round, circular, complete
熊	xióng a bear, brilliant, bright, surname	替	tì change, replace, substitute for	休	xiū rest, stop, retire, do not!
材	cái material, stuff, timber, talent	挑	tiāo a load carried on the shoulders, to carry	侠	xiá chivalrous person, knight-errant
鸡	jī chicken	累	léi bind, wind about, link, join	互	hù mutually, reciprocally
掌	zhǎng palm of hand, sole of foot, paw	念	niàn think of, recall, study	米	mǐ hulled or husked uncooked rice
伴	bàn companion, comrade, partner, accompany	辅	fǔ cheek bone, protective, assist	降	jiàng descend, fall, drop, lower, down
豪	háo brave, heroic, chivalrous	篮	lán basket	洗	xǐ wash, rinse, clean, purify
健	jiàn strong, robust, healthy, strength	饭	fàn cooked rice, food, meal	怜	lián pity, sympathize
疯	fēng crazy, insane, mentally ill	宏	hóng wide, spacious, great, vast	困	kùn be tired, sleepy
址	zhǐ site, location, land for house	兮	xī exclamatory particle	操	cāo conduct, run, control, manage
临	lín draw near, approach, descend	骗	piàn swindle, cheat out of, defraud	咧	liě stretch mouth, grimace, grin
药	yào drugs, pharmaceuticals, medicine	绿	lǜ green, chlorine	尼	ní Buddhist nun, transliteration

蔡	cài — surname, species of tortoise	玉	yù — jade, precious stone, gem	辛	xīn — bitter, toilsome, laborious, 8th heavenly stem
辈	bèi — generation, lifetime, class	敏	mǐn — fast, quick, clever, smart	减	jiǎn — decrease, subtract, diminish
彼	bǐ — that, there, those	街	jiē — street, road, thoroughfare	聚	jù — assemble, meet together, collect
郎	láng — gentleman, young man, husband	泡	pào — bubbles, suds, blister, soak	恨	hèn — hatred, dislike, resent, hate
缩	suō — contract, draw in, reduce	枢	shū — door hinge, pivot, center of power	碰	pèng — collide, bump into
采	cǎi — gather, collect, pick, select	默	mò — silent, quiet, still, dark	婆	pó — old woman, grandmother
股	gǔ — thighs, haunches, rump, share	童	tóng — child, boy, servant boy, virgin	符	fú — i.d. tag, tally, symbol, charm
抽	chōu — draw out, pull out, sprout	获	huò — harvest, cut grain	宇	yǔ — house, building, structure, eaves
废	fèi — abrogate, terminate, discard	赢	yíng — win, surplus, gain, profit	肯	kěn — willing, consent to, permit
砍	kǎn — hack, chop, cut, fell	钢	gāng — steel, hard, strong, tough	欧	ōu — used in transliterating non-Chinese words
届	jiè — numerary adjunct for time, term	禁	jìn — restrict, prohibit, forbid	苍	cāng — blue, green
脱	tuō — take off, peel off, strip	渐	jiàn — gradually	仙	xiān — Taoist super-being, transcendent, immortal
泪	lèi — tears, weep, cry	触	chù — touch, butt, ram, gore	途	tú — way, road, path, journey, course
财	cái — wealth, valuables, riches	箱	xiāng — case, box, chest, trunk	厌	yàn — dislike, detest, reject, satiate
籍	jí — record, register, list, census	冰	bīng — ice, ice-cold	涛	tāo — large waves
订	dìng — draw up agreement, arrange	哭	kū — weep, cry, wail	稳	wěn — stable, firm, solid, steady

析	xī	split wood, break apart, divide
杰	jié	hero, outstanding, remarkable
坚	jiān	hard, strong, firm, resolute
桥	qiáo	bridge, beam, crosspiece
懒	lǎn	lazy, languid, listless
贤	xián	virtuous, worthy, good, able
丝	sī	silk, fine thread, wire, strings
露	lù	dew, bare, open, exposed
森	sēn	forest, luxuriant vegetation
危	wēi	dangerous, precarious, high
占	zhān	divine, observe, versify
茶	chá	tea
惯	guàn	habit, custom, habitually, usually
尘	chén	dust, dirt, ashes, cinders
布	bù	cotton cloth, textiles, linen
爸	bà	father, papa
阶	jiē	stairs, steps, rank, degree
夏	xià	summer, great, grand, big
谊	yí	friendship, appropriate, suitable
瓶	píng	jug, pitcher, vase, jar, bottle
哩	lī	mile
惨	cǎn	sad, pitiful, wretched, cruel
械	jiè	weapons, implements, instruments
隐	yǐn	hide, conceal, hidden, secret
丰	fēng	abundant, lush, bountiful, plenty
旅	lǚ	trip, journey, travel, traveler
椰	yé	palm tree, coconut palm
亡	wáng	death, destroyed, lose, perish
汽	qì	steam, vapor, gas
贝	bèi	sea shell, money, currency
娘	niáng	mother, young girl, woman, wife
寒	hán	cold, wintry, chilly
遭	zāo	come across, meet with, encounter
吹	chuī	blow, puff, brag, boast
暑	shǔ	hot
珍	zhēn	precious, valuable, rare
零	líng	zero, fragment, fraction
刊	kān	publication, periodical, publish
邮	yóu	postal, mail, post office
村	cūn	village, hamlet, uncouth, vulgar
乃	nǎi	then, really, indeed, as it turned out, after all
予	yú	I, me, to give
赖	lài	rely, depend on, accuse falsely
摇	yáo	wag, swing, wave, shake, scull
纳	nà	admit, take, receive, accept
烟	yān	smoke, soot, opium, tobacco, cigarettes
伦	lún	normal human relationships
尾	wěi	tail, extremity, end, stern

狼 láng — wolf	浮 fú — to float, drift, waft, to exceed, superfluous	骨 gǔ — bone, skeleton, frame, framework
杯 bēi — cup, glass	隔 gé — separate, partition	洪 hóng — vast, immense, flood, deluge
织 zhī — weave, knit, organize, unite	询 xún — inquire into, ask about, consult	振 zhèn — raise, excite, arouse action
忽 hū — suddenly, abruptly, neglect	索 suǒ — large rope, cable, rules, laws, to demand	惠 huì — favor, benefit, confer kindness
峰 fēng — peak, summit, hump of camel	席 xí — seat, mat, take seat, banquet	喵 miāo — the mew of the cat
胡 hú — beard, mustache, whiskers	租 zū — rent, lease, rental, tax	款 kuǎn — item, article, clause, fund
扰 rǎo — disturb, annoy, agitate	企 qǐ — plan a project, stand on tiptoe	刺 cì — stab, prick, irritate, prod
芳 fāng — fragrant, virtuous, beautiful	鼠 shǔ — rat, mouse, KangXi radical 208	折 zhé — break off, snap, bend
频 pín — frequently, again and again	冒 mòu — risk, brave, dare	痴 chī — foolish, stupid, dumb, silly
阴 yīn — female' principle, dark, secret	哲 zhé — wise, sagacious, wise man, sage	针 zhēn — needle, pin, tack, acupuncture
伊 yī — third person pronoun, he, she, this, that	寂 jì — still, silent, quiet, desolate	嘴 zuǐ — mouth, lips
倚 yǐ — rely on, depend on, lean heavily	霸 bà — rule by might rather than right	扬 yáng — scatter, spread, praise
沉 chén — sink, submerge, addicted to	悔 huǐ — repent, show remorse, regret	虫 chóng — worms, insects
菜 cài — vegetables, dish, order, food	距 jù — distance, bird's spur	复 fù — cover, tip over, return, reply
鼓 gǔ — drum, beat, top, strike	摩 mó — rub, scour, grind, friction	郑 zhèng — state in today's Henan, surname
庄 zhuāng — village, hamlet, villa, surname	副 fù — assist, supplement, assistant	页 yè — page, sheet, leaf, rad. no. 181

烧	shāo — burn, bake, heat, roast	弱	ruò — weak, fragile, delicate	暂	zàn — temporary
剩	shèng — leftovers, residue, remains	豆	dòu — beans, peas, bean-shaped	探	tàn — find, locate, search, grope for
耐	nài — endure, bear, resist, patient	祖	zǔ — ancestor, forefather, grandfather	遍	biàn — everywhere, all over, throughout
萧	xiāo — common artemisia, dejected	握	wò — grasp, hold fast, take by hand	愁	chóu — anxiety, to worry about, be anxious
龟	guī — turtle or tortoise, cuckold	哀	āi — sad, mournful, pitiful, pity	发	fǎ — hair
延	yán — delay, postpone, defer	库	kù — armory, treasury, storehouse	隆	lóng — prosperous, plentiful, abundant
盟	méng — swear, oath, covenant, alliance	傻	shǎ — foolish, silly, stupid, an imbecile	眉	méi — eyebrows, upper margin of book
固	gù — to become solid, solidify, strength	秘	mì — secret, mysterious, abstruse	卷	juàn — scroll, curl, make a comeback
搭	dā — join together, attach to, add to	昭	zhāo — bright, luminous, illustrious	宁	zhù — repose, serenity, peace, peaceful
托	tuō — to hold up with palm, to support, rely on	辩	biàn — dispute, argue, debate, discuss	复	fù — cover, tip over, return, reply
吵	chǎo — argue, dispute, disturb, annoy	耳	ěr — ear, merely, only, handle	闲	xián — peaceful, tranquil, calm
拨	bō — move, dispel, distribute, plectrum	沈	shěn — juice, liquid, water, leak, pour	升	shēng — arise, go up, hoist, advance
胖	pàng — fat, obese, fatty	丁	dīng — male adult, robust, vigorous, 4th heavenly stem	妙	miào — mysterious, subtle, exquisite
残	cán — injure, spoil, oppress, broken	违	wéi — disobey, violate, defy, be apart from	稍	shāo — little, slightly, rather
媒	méi — go-between, matchmaker, medium	忧	yōu — sad, grieved, grief, melancholy	销	xiāo — melt, fuse, market, sell, to pass time, finish
恩	ēn — kindness, mercy, charity	颜	yán — face, facial appearance	船	chuán — ship, boat, vessel

奈	nài	but, how, bear, stand, endure	映	yìng	project, reflect light	井	jǐng	well, mine shaft, pit
拼	pīn	join together, link, incorporate	屋	wū	house, room, building, shelter	乘	chéng	ride, ascend, avail oneself of
京	jīng	capital city	藉	jiè	mat, pad, rely on, pretext	洞	dòng	cave, grotto, ravine, hole
川	chuān	stream, river, flow, boil	宪	xiàn	constitution, statute, law	拟	nǐ	draft, intend, plan, propose
寝	qǐn	sleep, rest, bed chamber	塞	sāi	stop up, block, seal, cork, pass, frontier	倍	bèi	times, fold, multiple times
户	hù	door, family, household	摆	bǎi	put, place, display, swing, sway	桌	zhuō	table, desk, stand
域	yù	district, region, boundary, land	劳	láo	labor, toil, do manual work	赚	zhuàn	make money, earn, gain, profit
皇	huáng	royal, imperial, ruler, superior	逃	táo	escape, flee, abscond, dodge	鸿	hóng	species of wild swan, vast
横	héng	across, horizontal, lateral	牙	yá	tooth, molars, teeth, serrated	拖	tuō	drag, tow, haul, delay, prolong
齐	qí	even, uniform, of equal length	农	nóng	agriculture, farming, farmer	滚	gǔn	turn, roll, rotate, boil
障	zhàng	separate, shield, barricade	搬	bān	transfer, move, remove, shift	奶	nǎi	milk, woman's breasts, nurse
乌	wū	crow, rook, raven, black, dark	了	liǎo	to finish, particle of completed action	松	sōng	lax, loose, loosen, relax
戴	dài	wear on top, support	谱	pǔ	register, list, table, musical score	酷	kù	strong, stimulating, very
棋	qí	chess, any game similar to chess	吓	xià	scare, frighten, intimidate	摸	mō	gently touch with hand, caress
额	é	forehead, tablet, plaque, fixed	瓜	guā	melon, gourd, cucumber, rad. 97	役	yì	service, a servant, laborer, to serve
怨	yuàn	hatred, enmity, resentment	染	rǎn	dye, be contagious, infect	迫	pò	coerce, force, compel, urgent

醉	zuì — intoxicated, drunk, addicted to	锁	suǒ — lock, padlock, shackles, chains	震	zhèn — shake, quake, tremor, excite
床	chuáng — bed, couch, framework, chassis	闹	nào — quarrel, dispute hotly	佩	pèi — belt ornament, pendant, wear at waist
牠	tuō — it, polled cattle	徐	xú — slowly, quietly, calmly, composed, dignified	尺	chǐ — Chinese measure approx. 'foot'
干	gàn — trunk of tree or of human body	潮	cháo — tide, moist, wet, damp, flow	帽	mào — hat, cap, cap-like tops
盛	shèng — abundant, flourishing, contain, fill	孙	sūn — grandchild, descendent, surname	屁	pì — break wind, fart, buttocks
净	jìng — clean, pure, cleanse	凯	kǎi — triumphant, triumph, victory	撞	zhuàng — knock against, bump into, collide
迴	huí — revolve, rotate, curving, zigzag	损	sǔn — diminish, impair, injure	伙	huǒ — companion, colleague, utensils
牵	qiān — drag, pull, lead by hand	厉	lì — whetstone, grind, sharpen, whet	惑	huò — confuse, mislead, baffle, doubt
羊	yáng — sheep, goat, KangXi radical 123	冬	dōng — winter, 11th lunar month	桃	táo — peach, marriage, surname
舰	jiàn — warship	眠	mián — close eyes, sleep, hibernate	伍	wǔ — five, company of five, troops
溪	xī — mountain stream, creek	飘	piāo — whirlwind, cyclone, floating	泰	tài — great, exalted, superior, big
宋	sòng — Song dynasty, surname	圈	quān — to circle, a circle, corral	竞	jìng — contend, vie, compete
闪	shǎn — flash, avoid, dodge, evade	纵	zòng — indulge in, give free reign to	崇	chóng — esteem, honor, revere, venerate
滑	huá — slip, slide, slippery, polished	乙	yǐ — second, 2nd heavenly stem	俗	sú — social customs, vulgar, unrefined
浅	qiǎn — shallow, not deep, superficial	莲	lián — lotus, water lily, paradise	紫	zǐ — purple, violet, amethyst, surname
沟	gōu — ditch, drain, narrow waterway	旋	xuán — revolve, move in orbit, return	摄	shè — take in, absorb, act as deputy, administer, assist

聪	cōng — intelligent, clever, bright	庭	tíng — courtyard, spacious hall or yard	麦	mài — wheat, barley, oats, KangXi radical number 199
描	miáo — copy, trace, sketch, depict	妨	fáng — interfere with, impede, obstruct	勒	lè — strangle, tighten
仪	yí — ceremony, rites gifts, admire	陪	péi — accompany, be with, keep company	榜	bǎng — placard, list of successful exam candidates
板	bǎn — boss, the owner, person in charge	慕	mù — long for, desire, admire	耀	yào — shine, sparkle, dazzle, glory
献	xiàn — offer, present, show, display	审	shěn — examine, investigate, judge	蟹	xiè — crab, brachyura
巷	xiàng — alley, lane	谅	liàng — excuse, forgive, guess, presume	姊	zǐ — elder sister
逐	zhú — chase, expel, one by one	踏	tà — step on, trample, tread on, walk	岸	àn — bank, shore, beach, coast
葛	gě — edible bean, surname	卧	wò — lie down, crouch	洽	qià — to blend with, be in harmony, to penetrate
寞	mò — silent, still, lonely, solitary	邦	bāng — nation, country, state	藤	téng — rattan, cane, creeper plant
拳	quán — fist, various forms of boxing	阻	zǔ — impede, hinder, obstruct, oppose	蝎	hé — scorpion
面	miàn — flour, dough, noodles	殊	shū — different, special, unusual	凭	píng — lean on, depend on, rely on
拒	jù — ward off with hand, defend	池	chí — pool, pond, moat, cistern	邪	xié — wrong, evil, depraved, vicious, perverse
航	háng — sail, navigate, ship, boat	驱	qū — spur a horse on, expel, drive away	裁	cái — cut out, decrease
翔	xiáng — soar, glide, hover, detailed	填	tián — fill in, fill up, make good	奥	ào — mysterious, obscure, profound
函	hán — correspondence, a case, a box	镇	zhèn — town, market place, suppress	几	jī — table
宽	kuān — broad, wide, spacious, vast	颇	pǒ — lean one side, very, rather	枪	qiāng — spear, lance, gun, rifle

遥	yáo — far away, distant, remote	穹	qióng — high and vast, elevated, arched	啪	pā — syllable
阅	yuè — examine	锋	fēng — point of spear, sharp point	砂	shā — sand, pebbles, gravel, gritty
恭	gōng — respectful, polite, reverent	塔	tǎ — tower, spire, tall building	贺	hè — congratulate, send present
魂	hún — soul, spirit	睛	jīng — eyeball, pupil of eye	逸	yì — flee, escape, break loose
旗	qí — banner, flag, streamer	萨	sà — transliteration of 'sat' in 'bodhisattva,' etc.	丸	wán — small round object, pellet, pill
厚	hòu — thick, substantial, greatly	斋	zhāi — vegetarian diet, study, to fast, abstain	芬	fēn — fragrance, aroma, perfume
革	gé — leather, animal hides, rad. 177	庸	yōng — usual, common, ordinary, mediocre	舒	shū — open up, unfold, stretch out, comfortable, easy
饮	yǐn — drink, swallow, kind of drink	闭	bì — shut, close, obstruct, block up	励	lì — strive, encourage
顿	dùn — pause, stop, bow, kowtow, arrange	仰	yǎng — raise the head to look, look up to, rely on	阁	gé — chamber, pavilion, cabinet
孟	mèng — first in series, great, eminent	昌	chāng — light of sun, good, proper	访	fǎng — visit, ask, inquire
绪	xù — end of thread, thread	裕	yù — abundant, rich, plentiful	勿	wù — must not, do not, without, never
州	zhōu — administrative division, state	阐	chǎn — explain, clarify, elucidate	抢	qiǎng — plunder, rob, take by force
扫	sǎo — sweep, clear away, exterminate	糊	hú — paste, stick on with paste	宙	zhòu — time as concept, infinite time
尝	cháng — taste, experience, experiment	菩	pú — herb, aromatic plant	赐	sì — give, bestow favors, appoint
赤	chì — red, communist, 'red', bare	喊	hǎn — shout, call out, yell, howl, cry	盗	dào — rob, steal, thief, bandit
擎	qíng — lift up, hold up, support	劝	quàn — recommend, advise, urge	奋	fèn — strive, exert effort, arouse

慈	cí	kind, charitable, benevolent	尽	jìn	exhaust, use up, deplete	污	wū	filthy, dirty, impure, polluted
狐	hú	species of fox	罚	fá	penalty, fine, punish, penalize	幽	yōu	quiet, secluded, tranquil, dark
准	zhǔn	rule, guideline, standard	兼	jiān	unite, combine, connect, and	尖	jiān	sharp, pointed, acute, keen
彰	zhāng	clear, manifest, obvious	灰	huī	ashes, dust, lime, mortar	番	fān	to take turns, a turn, a time, to repeat
衡	héng	measure, weigh, judge, consider	鲜	xiān	fresh, new, delicious, rare, few	扩	kuò	expand, enlarge, stretch
毫	háo	fine hair, measure of length	夸	kuā	exaggerate, brag, boast, flaunt	炮	pào	large gun, cannon, artillery
拆	chāi	to break up, split apart, rip open, to destroy	监	jiān	supervise, control, direct	栏	lán	railing, balustrade, animal pan
迟	chí	late, tardy, slow, delay	证	zhèng	proof, evidence, testify, verify	倾	qīng	upset, pour out, overflow
郁	yù	luxuriant, dense, thick, moody	汪	wāng	vast, extensive, deep, surname	纷	fēn	in disorder, scattered, tangled
托	tuō	to hold up with palm, to support, rely on	漏	lòu	leak, drip, funnel, hour glass	渡	dù	cross, ferry over, ferry
姑	gū	father's sister, husband's mother	秒	miǎo	beard of grain or corn, a second	吾	wú	i, my, our, resist, impede
窝	wō	nest, cave, den, hiding place	辆	liàng	numerary adjunct for vehicles	龄	líng	age, years
跌	diē	stumble, slip, fall down, stamp	浩	hào	great, numerous, vast, abundant	肥	féi	fat, plump, obese, fertile
兽	shòu	beast, animal, bestial	煞	shà	malignant deity, baleful, noxious, strike dead	抹	mǒ	smear, apply, wipe off, erase
酸	suān	tart, sour, acid, stiff, spoiled	税	shuì	taxes, revenue, duty, tax	陷	xiàn	submerge, sink, plunge, trap
谷	gǔ	corn, grain, cereal, lucky	冲	chōng	rush against, charge ahead	杜	dù	stop, prevent, restrict, surname

胸	xiōng breast, bosom, chest, thorax	甘	gān sweetness, sweet, tasty	胞	bāo womb, placenta, fetal membrane
诞	dàn to bear children, give birth, birth	岂	qǐ how? what?	辞	cí words, speech, expression, phrase
墙	qiáng wall	凉	liáng cool, cold, disheartened	碎	suì break, smash, broken, busted
晶	jīng crystal, clear, bright, radiant	邱	qiū surname, hill, mound, grave	逻	luó patrol, inspect, watch
脆	cuì crisp, fragile, frail, brittle	喷	pēn spurt, blow out, puff out	玫	méi rose
娃	wá baby, doll, pretty girl	培	péi bank up with dirt, cultivate	咱	zán us
潜	qián hide, hidden, secret, latent	祥	xiáng good luck, good omen, happiness	筑	zhú build, erect, building
孔	kǒng opening, hole, orifice, great	柏	bó cypress, cedar	叭	bā trumpet
邀	yāo invite, welcome, meet, intercept	犹	yóu like, similar to, just like, as	妻	qī wife
估	gū merchant, estimate, guess, presume	荒	huāng wasteland, desert, uncultivated	袋	dài pocket, bag, sack, pouch
径	jìng narrow path, diameter, direct	垃	lā garbage, refuse, waste	傲	ào proud, haughty, overbearing
淑	shú good, pure, virtuous, charming	圾	jí garbage, rubbish, shaking, danger	旦	dàn dawn, morning, day
亿	yì hundred million, many	截	jié cut off, stop, obstruct, intersect	币	bì currency, coins, legal tender
羽	yǔ feather, plume, wings, rad. 124	妇	fù married women, woman, wife	泥	ní mud, mire, earth, clay, plaster
欺	qī cheat, doublecross, deceive	弦	xián string, hypotenuse, crescent	筹	chóu chip, tally, token, raise money
舍	shě discard, give up willingly, give alms	忌	jì jealous, envious, fear	串	chuàn string, relatives, conspire

伸	shēn — extend, stretch out, open up, trust	喇	lǎ — horn, bugle, lama, final particle	耻	chǐ — shame, humiliation, ashamed
繁	fán — complicated, complex, difficult	廖	liào — surname, name of an ancient state	逛	guàng — ramble, stroll, roam, wander
劲	jìng — strong, unyielding, tough, powerful	臭	chòu — smell, stink, emit foul odor	鲁	lǔ — foolish, stupid, rash, vulgar
壮	zhuàng — big, large, robust, name of tribe	捕	bǔ — arrest, catch, seize	穷	qióng — poor, destitute, impoverished
拔	bá — uproot, pull out	丑	chǒu — ugly looking, homely, disgraceful	莉	lì — white jasmine
糟	zāo — sediment, dregs, pickle	炸	zhà — to fry in oil, to scald, to explode	坡	pō — slope, bank, hillside
腿	tuǐ — legs, thighs	坦	tǎn — flat, smooth, self-possessed	怒	nù — anger, rage, passion, angry
甜	tián — sweet, sweetness	韩	hán — fence, surname, Korea	缓	huǎn — slow, leisurely, to postpone, delay
悉	xī — know, learn about, comprehend	扯	chě — rip up, tear down, raise, haul	割	gē — cut, divide, partition, cede
艾	ài — artemisia, mugwort, translit.	胎	tāi — unborn child, embryo, fetus	恒	héng — constant, regular, persistent
玲	líng — tinkling of jade	朵	duǒ — cluster of flowers, earlobe	泉	quán — spring, fountain, wealth, money
汤	tāng — hot water, soup, gravy, broth	猛	měng — violent, savage, cruel, bold	驾	jià — to drive, sail, fly, a cart, carriage
幼	yòu — infant, young child, immature	坪	píng — level ground, Japanese measure	巫	wū — wizard, sorcerer, witch, shaman
弯	wān — bend, curve	胆	dǎn — gall bladder, bravery, courage	昏	hūn — dusk, nightfall, twilight, dark
鞋	xié — shoes, footwear in general	怡	yí — harmony, pleasure, joy, be glad	吐	tǔ — vomit, spew out, cough up
唐	táng — Tang dynasty, Chinese	悠	yōu — long, far, remote, distant, liesurely	盾	dùn — shield, dutch guilder, Indonesia

跃	yuè	skip, jump, frolic
鑑	jiàn	mirror, looking glass, reflect
逝	shì	pass away, die
召	zhào	imperial decree, summon
晨	chén	early morning, daybreak
痴	chī	foolish, stupid, dumb, silly
轩	xuān	carriage, high, wide, balcony
浓	nóng	thick, strong, concentrated
剪	jiǎn	scissors, cut, divide, separate
暖	nuǎn	warm, genial
症	zhēng	obstruction of bowels
碍	ài	obstruct, hinder, block, deter
蜜	mì	honey, sweet, nectar
赋	fù	tax, give, endow, army, diffuse
缴	jiǎo	deliver, submit, hand over
戒	jiè	warn, caution, admonish
侵	qīn	invade, encroach upon, raid
泽	zé	marsh, swamp, grace, brilliance, damp
彦	yàn	elegant, handsome, learned
吕	lǚ	surname, a musical note
辨	biàn	distinguish, discriminate
瑰	guī	extraordinary, fabulous, rose
勤	qín	industrious, diligent, attentive
悟	wù	to apprehend, realize, become aware
逼	bī	compel, pressure, force, bother
躲	duǒ	hide, secrete, avoid, escape
挡	dǎng	obstruct, impede, stop, resist
亨	hēng	smoothly, progressing, no trouble
盼	pàn	look, gaze, expect, hope for
彬	bīn	cultivated, well-bred
捷	jié	win, victory, triumph
憾	hàn	to regret, remorse, dissatisfied
丹	dān	vermilion
薪	xīn	fuel, firewood, salary
后	hòu	behind, rear, after, descendents
碧	bì	jade, green, blue
植	zhí	plant, trees, plants, grow
钓	diào	fish, fishhook, tempt, lure
珠	zhū	precious stone, gem, jewel, pearl
磨	mó	grind, polish, rub, wear out, a millstone
玄	xuán	deep, profound, abstruse
洛	luò	river in Shanxi province, city
敝	bì	break, destroy, broken, tattered
逊	xùn	humble, modest, yield
姆	mǔ	child's governess, matron
壁	bì	partition wall, walls of a house
乏	fá	lack, poor
滴	dī	drip, drop of water

桑	sāng — mulberry tree, surname	菲	fēi — fragrant, luxuriant, the Philippines	嫌	xián — hate, detest, suspect, criticize
愉	yú — pleasant, delightful, please	爬	pá — crawl, creep, climb, scramble	恼	nǎo — angered, filled with hate
删	shān — to cut, delete, erase, to geld	叹	tàn — sigh, admire	抵	dǐ — resist, oppose, deny, off-set
棚	péng — tent, awning, booth, shed	摘	zhāi — pluck, pick, select, specify	蒋	jiǎng — surname, hydropyrum latifalium
箭	jiàn — arrow, type of bamboo	夕	xī — evening, night, dusk, slanted	翁	wēng — old man, father, father-in-law
牲	shēng — sacrificial animal, animal	迹	jī — search, track, trace	勉	miǎn — endeavor, make effort, urge
莱	lái — goosefoot, weed, fallow field	洁	jié — clean, purify, pure	贪	tān — greedy, covet, covetous
恰	qià — just, exactly, precisely, proper	曰	yuē — say, KangXi radical 73	侨	qiáo — sojourn, lodge
沧	cāng — blue, dark green, cold	咖	kā — coffee, a phonetic	唷	yō — final particle
扣	kòu — knock, strike, rap, tap, button	奔	bēn — run fast, flee, rush about, run	泳	yǒng — dive, swim
迹	jī — search, track, trace	涯	yá — shore, bank, water's edge	夺	duó — take by force, rob, snatch
抄	chāo — copy, confiscate, seize	疗	liáo — be healed, cured, recover	署	shǔ — public office
誓	shì — swear, pledge, oath	盃	bēi — glass, cup	骚	sāo — harass, bother, annoy, disturb, agitate, sad
翼	yì — wings, fins on fish, shelter	屠	tú — butcher, slaughter, massacre	咪	mī — sound of cat, cat's meow, meter, (Cant.) don't!
雾	wù — fog, mist, vapor, fine spray	涉	shè — ford stream, wade across	锺	zhōng — (surname)
踢	tī — kick	谋	móu — plan, scheme, stratagem	牺	xī — sacrifice, give up, sacrificial

焦	jiāo	burned, scorched, anxious, vexed
涵	hán	soak, wet, tolerate, be lenient
础	chǔ	foundation stone, plinth
绕	rào	entwine, wind around, surround
俱	jù	all, together, accompany
霹	pī	thunder, crashing thunder
唬	hǔ	to intimidate, to scare
氏	shì	clan, family, mister
彻	chè	penetrate, pervade, penetrating
吝	lìn	stingy, miserly, parsimonious
曼	màn	long, extended, vast, beautiful
寿	shòu	old age, long life, lifespan
粉	fěn	powder, face powder, plaster
廉	lián	upright, honorable, honest
炎	yán	flame, blaze, hot
祸	huò	misfortune, calamity, disaster
耗	hào	consume, use up, waste, squander
炮	pào	large gun, cannon, artillery
啡	pēi	morphine, coffee
肚	dù	belly, abdomen, bowels
贡	gòng	offer tribute, tribute, gifts
鼻	bí	nose, first, KangXi radical 209
挖	wā	dig, dig out, gouge out, scoop
貌	mào	countenance, appearance
捐	juān	contribute, give up, renounce
融	róng	melt, fuse, blend, harmonize
筋	jīn	muscles, tendons
云	yún	clouds, Yunnan province
稣	sū	revive, to rise again, collect
捡	jiǎn	to pick up
饱	bǎo	eat heartily, eat one's fill
铃	líng	bell
雳	lì	thunderclap, crashing thunder
鸣	míng	cry of bird or animal, make sound
奉	fèng	offer, receive, serve, respect
燃	rán	burn, light fire, ignite
饰	shì	decorate, ornament, adorn, to deceive
绘	huì	draw, sketch, paint
黎	lí	surname, numerous, many, black
恢	huī	restore, big, great, immense, vast
瞧	qiáo	glance at, look at, see
茫	máng	vast, boundless, widespread
幅	fú	piece, strip, breadth of, hem
迪	dí	enlighten, advance, progress
柳	liǔ	willow tree, pleasure
瑜	yú	flawless gem or jewel
矛	máo	spear, lance, KangXi radical 110
吊	diào	condole, mourn, pity, hang

侯	hóu — marquis, lord, target in archery	玛	mǎ — agate, cornelian	撑	chēng — prop up, support, brace, to push off
薄	bó — thin, slight, weak, poor, stingy	敦	dūn — esteem, honest, candid, sincere	挤	jǐ — crowd, squeeze, push against
墨	mò — ink, writing	琪	qí — type of jade	凌	líng — pure, virtuous, insult, maltreat
侧	cè — side, incline, slant, lean	枫	fēng — maple tree	嗨	hǎi — hi
梯	tī — ladder, steps, stairs, lean	梁	liáng — bridge, beam, rafters, surname	廷	tíng — court
儒	rú — Confucian scholar	咬	yǎo — bite, gnaw	岚	lán — mountain mist, mountain haze
览	lǎn — look at, inspect, perceive	兔	tù — rabbit, hare	怖	bù — terror, fear, frighten, terrified
稿	gǎo — draft, manuscript, rough copy	齿	chǐ — teeth, gears, cogs, age, KangXi radical 211	狱	yù — prison, jail, case, lawsuit
爷	yé — father, grandfather	迈	mài — take a big stride, pass by	闷	mèn — gloomy, depressed, melancholy
乔	qiáo — tall, lofty, proud, stately	姿	zī — one's manner, carriage, bearing	踪	zōng — footprints, traces, tracks
宾	bīn — guest, visitor, surname, submit	家	jiā — house, home, residence, family	弘	hóng — enlarge, expand, liberal, great
韵	yùn — rhyme, vowel	岭	lǐng — mountain ridge, mountain peak	咦	yí — expression of surprise
裤	kù — trousers, pants	壳	ké — casing, shell, husk, hull, skin	孝	xiào — filial piety, obedience, mourning
仇	chóu — enemy, hate, hatred, enmity	誉	yù — fame, reputation, praise	妮	nī — maid, servant girl, cute girl
惧	jù — fear, be afraid of, dread	促	cù — urge, press, hurry, close	驶	shǐ — sail, drive, pilot, fast, quick
疼	téng — aches, pains, be fond of, love	凶	xiōng — culprit, murder, bad, sad	粗	cū — rough, thick, course, rude

耍	shuǎ frolic, play, amuse, play with	糕	gāo cakes, pastry	仲	zhòng middle brother, go between, mediator, surname
裂	liè split, crack, break open, rend	吟	yín sing, hum, recite, type of poetry	陀	tuó steep bank, rough terrain
赌	dǔ bet, gamble, wager, compete	爵	jué feudal title or rank	哉	zāi final exclamatory particle
亏	kuī lose, fail, damage, deficient	锅	guō cooking-pot, saucepan	刷	shuā brush, clean with brush, scrub
旭	xù rising sun, brilliance, radiant	晴	qíng clear weather, fine weather	蝶	dié butterfly
阔	kuò broad, ample, wide, be apart	洩	xiè leak, drip, vent or release	顽	wán obstinate, stubborn, recalcitrant
牧	mù tend cattle, shepherd	契	qì deed, contract, bond, engrave	轰	hōng rumble, explosion, blast
羞	xiū disgrace, shame, ashamed, shy	十	shí accounting form of the numeral ten	锦	jǐn brocade, tapestry, embroidered
逆	nì disobey, rebel, rebel, traitor	堕	duò fall, sink, let fall, degenerate	夹	jiā be wedged or inserted between
枝	zhī branches, limbs, branch off	瓦	wǎ tile, earthenware pottery, girl	舟	zhōu boat, ship, KangXi radical 137
悦	yuè pleased	惹	rě irritate, vex, offend, incite	疏	shū neglect, careless, lax
锐	ruì sharp	翘	qiáo turn up, lift, elevate, raise	哎	āi interjection of surprise
综	zòng arrange threads for weaving	纲	gāng heavy rope, hawser, main points	扇	shàn fan, door panel
驻	zhù to be stationed at, reside at, to stop	屏	píng folding screen, shield	堪	kān adequately capable of, worthy of
弥	mí extensive, full, fill, complete	贯	guàn a string of 1000 coins, to go through	愚	yú stupid, doltish, foolish
抬	tái lift, carry	靖	jìng pacify, appease, calm, peaceful	狠	hěn vicious, cruel, severely, extreme

饼	bǐng	rice-cakes, biscuits	凝	níng	coagulate, congeal, freeze	邻	lín	neighbor, neighborhood
擦	cā	wipe, scrub, rub, scour, brush	滋	zī	grow, multiply, increase, thrive	坤	kūn	earth, feminine, female
蛙	wā	frog	灾	zāi	calamity, disaster, catastrophe	莎	shā	kind of sedge grass, used anciently for raincoats
毅	yì	resolute, decisive, firm, persist	卒	zú	soldier, servant, at last, finally	汝	rǔ	you
赠	zèng	give present, bestow, confer	抛	pāo	throw (away), abandon, reject	秦	qín	feudal state of Qin, the Qin dynasty
辱	rù	humiliate, insult, abuse	涂	tú	smear, daub, apply, spread, paint	披	pī	wear, split, crack
允	yǔn	to grant, to allow, to consent	侦	zhēn	spy, reconnoiter, detective	欲	yù	desire, want, long for, intend
夥	huǒ	companion, partner, assistant	朗	lǎng	clear, bright, distinct	笛	dí	bamboo flute, whistle
劫	jié	take by force, coerce, disaster	魅	mèi	kind of forest demon, elf	钦	qīn	respect, admire, respectful
慰	wèi	comfort, console, calm	荷	hé	lotus, water lily, holland	挺	tǐng	to stand upright, straighten, rigid
矣	yǐ	particle of completed action	迅	xùn	quick, hasty, rapid, sudden	禅	chán	contemplation (dhyana), to level ground for altar
迁	qiān	move, shift, change, transfer	鹿	lù	deer, surname, KangXi radical 198	秤	chèng	balance, scale, steelyard
彭	péng	name of ancient country, surname	肩	jiān	shoulders, to shoulder, bear	赞	zàn	help, support, assist, aid
丙	bǐng	third, 3rd heavenly stem	鹅	é	goose	痕	hén	scar, mark, trace
液	yè	sap, juice, liquid, fluid	涨	zhǎng	rise in price	巡	xún	patrol, go on circuit, cruise
烤	kǎo	bake, roast, toast, cook	贱	jiàn	mean, low, cheap, worthless	丈	zhàng	unit of length equal 3.3 meters, gentleman

趋	qū	hasten, hurry, be attracted to	沿	yán	follow course, go along	滥	làn	flood, overflow, excessive
措	cuò	place, collect, arrange, employ	么	mo	interrogative final particle, insignificant	扭	niǔ	turn, twist, wrench, seize, grasp
捉	zhuō	grasp, clutch, catch, seize	碗	wǎn	bowl, small dish	炉	lú	fireplace, stove, oven, furnace
脏	zāng	dirty, firm, fat	叔	shū	father's younger brother	秘	mì	secret, mysterious, abstruse
腰	yāo	waist, kidney	漠	mò	desert, aloof, indifferent, cool	翅	chì	wings, fin
余	yú	surplus, excess, remainder	胶	jiāo	glue, gum, resin, rubber	妥	tuǒ	satisfactory, appropriate
谣	yáo	sing, folksong, ballad, rumor	缸	gāng	earthen jug, crock, cistern	芒	máng	Miscanthus sinensis
陵	líng	hill, mound, mausoleum	雯	wén	cloud patterns, coloring of cloud	轨	guǐ	track, rut, path
虾	xiā	shrimp, prawn	寸	cùn	inch, small, tiny	呦	yōu	the bleating of the deer
洒	sǎ	sprinkle, splash, scatter, throw	贞	zhēn	virtuous, chaste, pure, loyal	蜂	fēng	bee, wasp, hornet
钻	zuàn	drill, bore, pierce, diamond	厕	cè	toilet, lavatory, mingle with	鹤	hè	crane, Grus species (various)
摔	shuāi	fall ground, stumble, trip	盒	hé	small box or case, casket	虫	chóng	worms, insects
氛	fēn	gas, vapor, air	悄	qiǎo	silent, quiet, still, anxious	霖	lín	long spell of rain, copious rain
愧	kuì	ashamed, conscience-stricken	斜	xié	slanting, sloping, inclined	尸	shī	corpse, carcass
循	xún	obey, comply with, follow	俩	liǎ	clever, skilled, two, pair	堡	bǎo	fort, fortress, town, village
旺	wàng	prosper, prosperous, increase	恶	è	evil, wicked, bad, foul	叉	cha	crotch, fork, prong

燕	yàn	swallow (bird), comfort, enjoy	津	jīn	ferry, saliva, ford	臣	chén	minister, statesman, official
丧	sāng	mourning, mourn, funeral	茂	mào	thick, lush, dense, talented	椅	yǐ	chair, seat
缠	chán	wrap, wind around, tie, bind	刑	xíng	punishment, penalty, law	脉	mò	blood vessels, veins, arteries
杉	shān	various species of pine and fir	泊	bó	anchor vessel, lie at anchor	撒	sǎ	release, cast away, let go, disperse, relax
递	dì	hand over, deliver, substitute	疲	pí	feel tired, be exhausted, weak	杆	gǎn	pole, stick, club, pole as unit
趁	chèn	take advantage of, avail oneself	欠	qiàn	owe, lack, be deficient, KangXi radical number 76	盈	yíng	fill, full, overflowing, surplus
晃	huǎng	bright, dazzling, to sway, shake	蛇	shé	snake	牡	mǔ	male of animals, bolt of door
慎	shèn	act with care, be cautious	粒	lì	grain, small particle	倦	juàn	be tired of, weary
溜	liū	slide, glide, slip, slippery	遵	zūn	obey, comply with, follow, honor	腐	fǔ	rot, decay, spoil, rotten
疾	jí	illness, disease, sickness, to hate	鸭	yā	duck, Anas species (various)	璃	lí	glass
牢	láo	prison, stable, pen, secure	劣	liè	bad, inferior, slightly	患	huàn	suffer, worry about, suffering
祂	tā	he	呈	chéng	submit, show, appear, petition	浑	hún	muddy, turbid, blend, merge, mix
剂	jì	medicinal preparation	妖	yāo	strange, weird, supernatural	玻	bō	glass
塑	sù	model in clay, sculpt, plastics	飙	biāo	whirlwind, stormy gale	伏	fú	crouch, crawl, lie hidden, conceal
弊	bì	evil, wrong, bad, criminal	扮	bàn	dress up, dress up as	侬	nóng	I, you, family name
渴	kě	thirsty, parched, yearn, pine	歪	wāi	slant, inclined, askewd, awry	苗	miáo	sprouts, Miao nationality

汗 hàn — perspiration, sweat	陶 táo — pottery, ceramics	栋 dòng — the main beams supporting a house
琳 lín — beautiful jade, gem	蓉 róng — hibiscus, Chengdu, Sichuan	埋 mái — bury, secrete, conceal
叡 ruì — astute, profound, shrewd	澎 péng — splatter	并 bìng — combine, annex
泣 qì — cry, sob, weep	腾 téng — fly, gallop, run, prance, rise	柯 kē — axe-handle, stalk, bough, surname
催 cuī — press, urge	畅 chàng — smoothly, freely, unrestrained	勾 gōu — hook, join, connect, entice
樱 yīng — cherry, cherry blossom	阮 ruǎn — ancient musical instrument; surname	斥 chì — to scold, upbraid, accuse, reproach
搜 sōu — search, seek, investigate	踩 cǎi — step on	返 fǎn — return, revert to, restore
坛 tán — an earthenware jar, a jug	垂 chuí — let down, suspend, hand, down	唤 huàn — call, summon, invite, be called
储 chǔ — to save money, store, reserve, an heir	贩 fàn — peddler, hawker, street merchant	匆 cōng — hastily, in haste, hurriedly
添 tiān — append, add to, increase	坑 kēng — pit, hole, bury, trap, harry	柴 chái — firewood, faggots, fuel
邓 dèng — surname	糖 táng — sugar, candy, sweets	昆 kūn — elder brother, descendants
暮 mù — evening, dusk, sunset, ending	柜 guì — cupboard, wardrobe, counter	娟 juān — beautiful, graceful
腹 fù — stomach, belly, abdomen, inside	煮 zhǔ — cook	泛 fàn — to drift, float, careless, reckless
稀 xī — rare, unusual, scarce, sparse	兹 zī — now, here, this, time, year	抑 yì — press down, repress, curb, hinder
携 xī — lead by hand, take with, carry	芭 bā — plantain or banana palm, fragrant	框 kuàng — frame, framework, door frame
彷 páng — like, resembling, resemble	罐 guàn — jar, jug, pitcher, pot	虹 hóng — rainbow

拷 kǎo — torture and interrogate, hit	萍 píng — duckweed, wandering, traveling	臂 bì — arm
袭 xí — raid, attack, inherit	叙 xù — express, state, relate, narrate	吻 wěn — kiss, the lips, coinciding
仿 fǎng — imitate, copy, as if	贼 zéi — thief, traitor	羯 jié — wether, castrated ram, deer skin
浴 yù — bathe, wash, bath	体 tǐ — body, group, class, body, unit	翠 cuì — color green, kingfisher
灿 càn — vivid, illuminating, bright	敲 qiāo — strike, beat, pound, hammer, rap	胁 xié — ribs, armpits, flank, threaten
侣 lǚ — companion, associate with	蚁 yǐ — ants	秩 zhì — order, orderly, salary, decade
佑 yòu — help, protect, bless	谨 jǐn — prudent, cautious, attentive	寡 guǎ — widowed, alone, friendless
岳 yuè — mountain peak, surname	赔 péi — indemnify, suffer loss	掩 yǎn — to cover (with the hand), shut, conceal, ambush
匙 chí — spoon, surname	曹 cáo — ministry officials, surname	纽 niǔ — knot, button, handle, knob, tie
晋 jìn — advance, increase, promote	喻 yù — metaphor, analogy, example, like	绵 mián — cotton wad, wool, soft, downy
咏 yǒng — sing, hum, chant	摊 tān — spread out, open, apportion	馨 xīn — fragrant, aromatic, distant fragrance
珊 shān — coral	孕 yùn — be pregnant, pregnancy	杰 jié — hero, outstanding, remarkable
拘 jū — restrain, seize, detain	哟 yo — ah, final particle	羡 xiàn — envy, admire, praise, covet
肤 fū — skin, superficial, shallow	肝 gān — liver	袍 páo — long gown, robe, cloak
罩 zhào — basket for catching fish, cover	叛 pàn — rebel, rebellion, rebellious	御 yù — defend, resist, hold out against
谜 mí — riddle, conundrum, puzzle	嫁 jià — to marry, give a daughter in marriage	庙 miào — temple, shrine, imperial court

肠	cháng	intestines, emotions, sausage
谎	huǎng	lie
潘	pān	surname, water in which rice has been rinsed
埔	bù	plain, arena, port, market
卜	bó	radish
占	zhān	divine, observe, versify
拦	lán	obstruct, impede, bar, hinder
煌	huáng	bright, shining, luminous
俄	é	sudden(ly), soon, Russian
札	zhá	letter, note, correspondence
骤	zòu	procedure, gallop, sudden(ly)
陌	mò	foot path between rice fields
澄	chéng	purify water by allowing sediment to settle
仓	cāng	granary, berth, sea
匪	fěi	bandits, robbers, gangsters
宵	xiāo	night, evening, dark
钮	niǔ	button, knob, surname
岗	gǎng	post, position
荡	dàng	pond, pool, wash away, cleanse
卸	xiè	lay down, retire from office
旨	zhǐ	purpose, aim, excellent
粽	zòng	dumpling made of glutinous rice
贸	mào	trade, barter, mixed, rashly
舌	shé	tongue, clapper of bell, KangXi radical 135
历	lì	take place, past, history
叮	dīng	exhort or enjoin repeatedly
咒	zhòu	curse, damn, incantation
钥	yào	key, lock
苹	pín	apple
祭	jì	sacrifice to, worship
屈	qū	bend, flex, bent, crooked, crouch
陋	lòu	narrow, crude, coarse, ugly
雀	què	sparrow
睹	dǔ	look at, gaze at, observe
媚	mèi	charming, attractive, flatter
娜	nuó	elegant, graceful, delicate
诱	yòu	persuade, entice, induce, guide
衷	zhōng	heart, from bottom of one's heart
菁	jīng	flower of leek family, turnip
殿	diàn	hall, palace, temple
撕	sī	rip, tear, buy cloth
蠢	chǔn	wriggle, stupid, silly, fat
惟	wéi	but, however, nevertheless, only
嚣	xiāo	be noisy, treat with contempt
踊	yǒng	leap, jump
跨	kuà	straddle, bestride, ride, carry
膀	bǎng	upper arm, shoulder, wing
筒	tǒng	thick piece of bamboo, pipe

纹	wén	line, streak, stripe, wrinkle	乳	rǔ	breast, nipples, milk, suckle	仗	zhàng	rely upon, protector, fight, war, weaponry
轴	zhóu	axle, axletree, pivot, axis	撤	chè	omit, remove, withdraw	潭	tán	deep pool, lake, deep, profound
佛	fó	Buddha, of Buddhism, merciful percon	桂	guì	cassia or cinnamon	愤	fèn	resent, hate, indignant
捧	pěng	hold up in two hands	袖	xiù	sleeve, put something in sleeve	埃	āi	fine dust, dirt
壹	yī	number one	赫	hè	bright, radiant, glowing	谦	qiān	humble, modest
汇	huì	collect, compile, assemble, hedgehog	魏	wèi	kingdom of Wei, surname	粹	cuì	pure, unadulterated, select
傅	fù	tutor, teacher, assist, surname	寮	liáo	shanty, hut, shack	猴	hóu	monkey, ape, monkey-like
衰	shuāi	decline, falter, decrease, weaken	辜	gū	crime, criminal offense	恳	kěn	sincere, earnest, cordial
桶	tǒng	pail, bucket, tub, cask, keg	吋	cùn	inch	衫	shān	shirt, robe, gown, jacket
瞬	shùn	wink, blink, in a wink, a flash	冻	dòng	freeze, cold, congeal, jelly	猎	liè	hunt, field sports
琼	qióng	jade, rare, precious, elegant	卿	qīng	noble, high officer	戚	qī	relative, be related to, sad
卓	zhuō	profound, brilliant, lofty	殖	zhí	breed, spawn, increase, prosper	泼	pō	pour, splash, water, sprinkle, violent, malignant
譬	pì	metaphor, simile, example	翰	hàn	writing brush, pen, pencil	刮	guā	to blow
斌	bīn	refined, having both appearance	枉	wǎng	useless, in vain, bent, crooked	庞	páng	disorderly, messy, huge, big
闽	mǐn	fujian province, a river, a tribe	宅	zhái	residence, dwelling, home, grave	麟	lín	female of Chinese unicorn
宰	zǎi	to slaughter, to rule	梭	suō	weaver's shuttle, go to and fro	纠	jiǎo	investigate, inspect

丛 cóng — bush, shrub, thicket, collection	澳 ào — inlet, bay, dock, bank	毙 bì — kill, die violent death
颖 yǐng — rice tassel, sharp point, clever	腔 qiāng — chest cavity, hollow in body	伫 zhù — wait, look towards, turn one's back on
躺 tǎng — lie down, recline	划 huà — delineate, painting, picture, drawing, draw	寺 sì — court, office, temple, monastery
炼 liàn — smelt, refine, distill, condense	胃 wèi — stomach, gizzard of fowl	昂 áng — rise, raise, proud, bold, upright
勋 xūn — meritorious deed, merits, rank	骄 jiāo — spirited horse, haughty	卑 bēi — humble, low, inferior, despise
蚂 mǎ — ant, leech	墓 mù — grave, tomb	冥 míng — dark, gloomy, night, deep
妄 wàng — absurd, foolish, reckless, false	董 dǒng — direct, supervise, surname	淋 lín — drip, soak, drench, perfectly
卢 lú — cottage, hut, surname, black	偿 cháng — repay, recompense, restitution	姻 yīn — relatives by marriage
砸 zá — smash, crush, break, pound, mash	践 jiàn — trample, tread upon, walk on	殷 yīn — many, great, abundant, flourishing
润 rùn — soft, moist, sleek, freshen	铜 tóng — copper, brass, bronze cuprum	盲 máng — blind, unperceptive, shortsighted
扎 zhā — pull up, pierce, struggle free	驳 bó — varicolored, variegated, mixed, contradict, argue	湿 shī — wet, moist, humid, damp, an illness
凑 còu — piece together, assemble	炒 chǎo — fry, saute, roast, boil, cook	尿 niào — urine, urinate
穴 xuè — cave, den, hole, rad. no. 116	蟑 zhāng — cockroach	拓 tuò — expand, open up, support or push
诡 guǐ — deceive, cheat, defraud, sly	谬 miù — error, exaggeration, erroneous	淫 yín — obscene, licentious, lewd
鼎 dǐng — large, three-legged bronze caldron	斩 zhǎn — cut, chop, sever, behead	尧 yáo — a legendary ancient emperor-sage
伪 wěi — false, counterfeit, bogus	饿 è — hungry, greedy for, hunger	驰 chí — go quickly or swiftly, hurry

蚊 wén — mosquito, gnat	瘟 wēn — epidemic, plague, pestilence	肢 zhī — human limbs, animal feet
挫 cuò — push down, chop down, grind	槽 cáo — trough, manger, vat, tank, groove, a distillery	扶 fú — support, help, protect, hold on
兆 zhào — omen, million, mega, also trillion. China	僧 sēng — Buddhist priest, monk, san of Sanskrit sangha	昧 mèi — obscure, dark, darken
螂 láng — mantis, dung beetle	匹 pǐ — bolt of cloth, counter for horses	芝 zhī — sesame
奸 jiān — adultery, debauchery, debauch	聘 pìn — engage, employ, betroth	眷 juàn — take interest in, care for
熙 xī — bright, splendid, glorious	猩 xīng — species of orangutan	痒 yǎng — itch
帖 tiē — invitation card, notice	贫 pín — poor, impoverished, needy	贿 huì — bribe, bribes, riches, wealth
扑 pū — pound, beat, strike, attack	笼 lóng — cage, cage-like basket	丘 qiū — hill, elder, empty, a name
颠 diān — top, peak, summit, upset	讶 yà — express surprise, be surprised	玮 wěi — type of jade, rare, valuable
尹 yǐn — govern, oversee, director	诇 xiòng — to spy, to give information, shrewd	柱 zhù — pillar, post, support, lean on
袁 yuán — robe, surname	漆 qī — varnish, lacquer, paint	毋 wú — do not, not, surname, rad. 80
辣 là — peppery, pungent, hot, cruel	棍 gùn — stick, cudgel, scoundrel	矩 jǔ — carpenter's square, ruler, rule
佐 zuǒ — assist, aid, second, subordinate	澡 zǎo — wash, bathe	渊 yuān — gulf, abyss, deep
痞 pǐ — dyspepsia, spleen infection	矮 ǎi — short, dwarf, low	戈 gē — halberd, spear, lance
勃 bó — suddenly, sudden, quick	吞 tūn — swallow, absorb, annex, engulf	肆 sì — indulge, excess, numeral four
抖 dǒu — tremble, shake, rouse, give shake	咳 ké — cough	亭 tíng — pavilion, erect

淘	táo — wash in sieve, weed out	穗	suì — ear of grain, tassel, Guangzhou	黏	nián — stick to, glutinous, sticky, glue
冈	gāng — ridge or crest of hill	歧	qí — fork of road, branching off	屑	xiè — bits, scraps, crumbs, fragments
拢	lǒng — collect, bring together	潇	xiāo — sound of beating wind and rain, light, ethereal	谐	xié — harmonize, agree, joke, jest
遣	qiǎn — send, dispatch, send off, exile	诊	zhěn — examine patient, diagnose	祈	qí — pray, entreat, beseech
霜	shuāng — frost, crystallized, candied	熬	áo — cook down, to boil, endure	饶	ráo — bountiful, abundant, plentiful
闯	chuǎng — rush in, burst in, charge in	婉	wǎn — amiable, congenial, restrained	致	zhì — delicate, fine, dense
雁	yàn — wild goose	觅	mì — seek, search	讽	fēng — recite, incant, satirize
膜	mò — membrane, to kneel and worship	挣	zhēng — to strive, endeavor, struggle, to earn	斤	jīn — a catty (approximately 500 g), an axe, keen
帆	fān — sail, boat	铺	pū — spread out, arrange, shop	瑟	sè — large stringed musical instrument, dignified
艇	tǐng — small boat, dugout, punt	壶	hú — jar, pot, jug, vase, surname	苑	yuàn — pasture, park, garden, mansion
悬	xuán — hang, suspend, hoist, be hung	詹	zhān — surname, talk too much, verbose	诠	quán — explain, expound, comment on
滤	lǜ — strain out, filter	稚	zhì — young, immature, childhood	辰	chén — early morning, 5th terrestrial branch
募	mù — levy, raise, summon, recruit	懿	yì — virtuous, admirable, esteemed	慨	kǎi — sigh, regret, generous
哼	hēng — hum, sing softly, groan, moan	汁	zhī — juice, liquor, fluid, sap, gravy, sauce	佬	lǎo — (Cant.) man, person, mature
纤	xiān — fine, delicate, minute, graceful	肃	sù — pay respects, reverently	遨	áo — ramble, roam, travel for pleasure
渔	yú — to fish, seize, pursue, surname	恕	shù — forgive, excuse, show mercy	蝴	hú — butterfly

垫	diàn	advance money, pay for another	昱	yù	bright light, sunlight, dazzling	竿	gān	bamboo pole, penis
缝	féng	sew, mend	蹈	dào	stamp feet, dance	鞭	biān	whip, whip, string of firecrackers
仆	pú	slave, servant, I	豫	yù	relaxed, comfortable, at ease	岩	yán	cliff, rocks, mountain
辐	fú	spokes of wheel	歹	dǎi	bad, vicious, depraved, wicked	甄	zhēn	to examine, discern, to grade, a surname
斑	bān	mottled, striped, freckle	淹	yān	drown, cover with liquid, steep	崎	qí	rough, uneven, jagged, rugged
骏	jùn	excellent horse, noble steed	薰	xūn	a medicinal herb, to cauterize	婷	tíng	pretty, attractive, graceful
宠	chǒng	favorite, concubine, favor	棵	kē	numerary adjunct for trees	弓	gōng	bow, curved, arched, KangXi radical number 57
犬	quǎn	dog, radical number 94	涂	tú	smear, daub, apply, spread, paint	刹	chà	temple
坎	kǎn	pit, hole, snare, trap, crisis	煎	jiān	fry in fat or oil, boil in water	螺	luó	spiral shell, conch, spiral
遮	zhē	cover, shield, protect	枯	kū	dried out, withered, decayed	台	tái	taiphoon
昔	xí	formerly, ancient, in beginning	瘾	yǐn	rash, addiction, craving, habit	蒂	dì	peduncle or stem of plants
坠	zhuì	fall down, drop, sink, go to ruin	唔	wú	hold in mouth, bite	瞎	xiā	blind, reckless, rash
筝	zhēng	stringed musical instrument, kite	唇	chún	lips	表	biǎo	a watch, clock
吁	xū	interjection 'Alas!', to sigh	冤	yuān	grievance, injustice, wrong	祷	dǎo	pray, entreat, beg, plead, prayer
甩	shuǎi	throw away, discard	伞	sǎn	umbrella, parasol, parachute	酱	jiàng	any jam-like or paste-like food
范	fàn	pattern, model, rule, law	焉	yān	thereupon, then, how? why? where?	娇	jiāo	seductive and loveable, tender

驼 tuó — a camel, humpbacked, to carry on the back	沦 lún — be lost, sink, be submerged	碳 tàn — carbon
沾 zhān — moisten, wet, soak, touch	抚 fǔ — pat, console, comfort, pacify	溶 róng — to melt, dissolve, overflowing with
叠 dié — repeat, duplicate, repetitious	几 jǐ — how many? how much?, a few, some	蜡 là — wax, candle, waxy, glazed
涌 yǒng — surge up, bubble up, gush forth	氧 yǎng — oxygen	娱 yú — pleasure, enjoyment, amusement
皓 hào — bright, luminous, clear, hoary	奴 nú — slave, servant	颓 tuí — ruined
嘎 gā — sound of laughter, bad, malevolent	趟 tàng — time, occasion, take journey	揭 jiē — raise, lift up, surname
当 dāng — sound of bells	剥 bō — peel, peel off, to shell, strip	垦 kěn — cultivate, reclaim, to farm land
狭 xiá — narrow, limited, narrow-minded, to pinch	魁 kuí — chief, leader, best, monstrous	坊 fāng — neighborhood, urban subdivision
盐 yán — variant of 塩 U+5869, salt	屎 shǐ — excrement, dung	郝 hǎo — surname, place in modern Shanxi
摧 cuī — destroy, break, injure	栗 lì — shiver, shudder, tremble, tremble	菊 jú — chrysanthemum
瘦 shòu — thin, emaciated, lean, meager	钧 jūn — unit of measure equivalent to thirty catties	匿 nì — hide, go into hiding
砖 zhuān — tile, brick	嘘 xū — exhale, blow out, deep sigh, hiss, praise	缚 fú — to tie
嘟 dū — sound of horn tooting	盆 pén — basin, tub, pot, bowl	债 zhài — debt, loan, liabilities
霞 xiá — rosy clouds	挽 wǎn — mourn, pull, draw	逍 xiāo — ramble, stroll, jaunt, loiter
畔 pàn — boundary path dividing fields	蕴 yùn — collect, gather, store, profound, (Budd.) skandha	颈 jǐng — neck, throat
获 huò — harvest, cut grain	畏 wèi — fear, dread, awe, reverence	喂 wèi — interjection to call attention

脾 **pí** spleen, pancreas, disposition	姬 **jī** beauty, imperial concubine	赴 **fù** go to, attend, be present
囊 **náng** bag, purse, sack, put in bag	噪 **zào** be noisy, chirp loudly	熄 **xí** put out, extinguish, quash
锡 **xí** tin, stannum, bestow, confer	诀 **jué** take leave of, bid farewell	肇 **zhào** begin, commence, originate
璋 **zhāng** jade plaything, jade ornament	晕 **yūn** halo in sky, fog, dizzy, faint	浊 **zhuó** muddy, turbid, dirty, filthy
伐 **fá** cut down, subjugate, attack	峡 **xiá** gorge, strait, ravine, isthmus	窃 **qiè** secretly, stealthily, steal, thief
枕 **zhěn** pillow	倘 **tǎng** if, supposing, in event of	慌 **huāng** nervous, panicky, frantic
垮 **kuǎ** be defeated, fail, collapse	帕 **pà** turban, kerchief, veil, wrap	莹 **yíng** lustre of gems, bright, lustrous
琦 **qí** gem, precious stone, jade	厢 **xiāng** side-room, wing, theatre box	渺 **miǎo** endlessly long, boundless, vast
脏 **zāng** dirty, firm, fat	削 **xuē** scrape off, pare, trim	锣 **luó** gong
虐 **nvè** cruel, harsh, oppressive	豔 **yàn** plump, voluptuous, beautiful	薇 **wéi** Osmunda regalis, a species of fern
霉 **méi** mildew, mold, moldy, mildewed	衍 **yǎn** overflow, spill over, spread out	腊 **là** year end sacrifice, dried meat
喧 **xuǎn** lively, noisy, clamor, talk loudly	娶 **qǔ** marry, take wife	遂 **suì** comply with, follow along, thereupon
睁 **zhēng** to open the eyes, stare	裙 **qún** skirt, apron, petticoat	韦 **wéi** tanned leather, surname
矢 **shǐ** arrow, dart, vow, swear	伺 **sì** serve, wait upon, attend, examine	钉 **dīng** nail, spike, pursue closely
婴 **yīng** baby, infant, bother	蓄 **xù** store, save, hoard, gather	奸 **jiān** adultery, debauchery, debauch
廿 **niàn** twenty, twentieth	堵 **dǔ** wall, stop, prevent, stop up	葬 **zàng** bury, inter

蓬 péng — type of raspberry, fairyland	鸦 yā — crow, raven, Corvus species (various)	挨 āi — near, close by, next to, towards, against
蕾 lěi — buds, unopened flowers	璇 xuán — fine jade	挚 zhì — sincere, warm, cordial, surname
券 quàn — certificate, ticket, title deeds	厨 chú — kitchen, closet, cupboard	醇 chún — rich, good as wine, pure, unmixed
呻 shēn — groan, moan, recite with intonation	霍 huò — quickly, suddenly, surname	剃 tì — shave
浆 jiāng — any thick fluid, starch, broth	葡 pú — grapes	暨 jì — and, attain, reach, confines
滨 bīn — beach, sea coast, river bank	履 lǚ — footwear, shoes, walk on, tread	捞 lāo — scoop out of water, dredge, fish
咕 gū — mumble, mutter, murmur, rumble	耕 gēng — plow, cultivate	棉 mián — cotton, cotton padded
烁 shuò — shine, glitter, sparkle	尉 wèi — officer, military rank	艰 jiān — difficult, hard, distressing
妓 jì — prostitute	棺 guān — coffin	鹏 péng — fabulous bird of enormous size
蒸 zhēng — steam, evaporate	癌 yán — cancer, marmoset	纬 wěi — woof, parallels of latitude
菌 jùn — mushroom, germ, microbe	撇 piě — discard, abandon, throw away	惩 chéng — punish, reprimand, warn
绑 bǎng — bind, tie, fasten	甫 fǔ — begin, man, father, great	崩 bēng — rupture, split apart, collapse
魄 pò — vigor, body, dark part of moon	拂 fú — shake off, brush away, dust	汰 tài — excessive, scour, wash out
氓 máng — people, subjects, vassals	歇 xiē — rest, stop, lodge	萝 luó — type of creeping plant, turnip
呋 fū — unclear, an expletive	萄 táo — grapes	蕃 fán — foreign things
曝 pù — sun, air in sun, expose or dry in the sun	疋 pǐ — roll, bolt of cloth, foot	胏 zǐ — meat

烛 zhú candle, taper, to shine, illuminate	腻 nì greasy, oily, dirty, smooth	襄 xiāng aid, help, assist, undress
妆 zhuāng to adorn oneself, dress up, use make-up	髓 suǐ bone marrow, essences, substances	朴 pú simple, honest, plain, rough
薯 shǔ yam, tuber, potato	颂 sòng laud, acclaim, hymn, ode	薛 xiē kind of marsh grass, feudal state
滩 tān bank, a sandbar, shoal, rapids	橘 jú orange, tangerine	贰 èr number two
嘲 cháo ridicule, deride, scorn, jeer at	叹 tàn sigh, admire	枚 méi stalk of shrub, trunk of tree
侮 wǔ insult, ridicule, disgrace	豹 bào leopard, panther, surname	巢 cháo nest, living quarter in tree
酬 chóu toast, reward, recompense	碑 bēi stone tablet, gravestone	翩 piān fly, flutter
蚕 cán silkworms	辽 liáo distant, far	矿 kuàng mine, mineral, ore
屡 lǚ frequently, often, again and again	谴 qiǎn reprimand, scold, abuse	卵 luǎn egg, ovum, roe, spawn
撰 zhuàn compose, write, compile	攀 pān climb, pull, hang on to	肌 jī muscle tissue, meat on bones
冯 féng surname, gallop, by dint of	宴 yàn to entertain, feast, a feast, banquet	盏 zhǎn small cup or container
坂 bǎn hillside farmland, slope	浦 pǔ bank of river, shore, surname	迦 jiā character for transliteration
颁 bān confer, bestow, publish, promulgate	炼 liàn smelt, refine, distill, condense	尬 gà limp, staggering gait, embarrass
胀 zhàng swell, inflate, expand	辟 pì law, rule, open up, develop	艘 sāo counter for ships, vessels
株 zhū numerary adjunct for trees, root	只 zhī single, one of pair, lone	湘 xiāng Hunan province
饲 sì raise animals, feed, nourish	爹 diē father, daddy	梨 lí pear, opera, cut, slash

喽	lou	used in onomatopoetic expressions	侍	shì	serve, attend upon, attendant, servant, samurai	疫	yì	epidemic, plague, pestilence
黯	àn	dark, black, sullen, dreary	并	bìng	combine, annex	铝	lǚ	aluminum
弗	fú	not, negative	爪	zhuǎ	claw, nail, talon, animal feet	鄙	bǐ	mean, low
钗	chāi	ornamental hairpin	栽	zāi	to cultivate, plant, to care for plants	狸	lí	fox
谘	zī	consult, confer, communicate in	柄	bǐng	handle, lever, knob, authority	悸	jì	fearful, apprehensive, perturbed
喉	hóu	throat, gullet, larynx, guttural	擅	shàn	monopolize, claim, arbitrarily, to dare	劈	pī	cut apart, split, chop
秉	bǐng	grasp, hold, bundle, authority	芷	zhǐ	angelica, type of iris	裸	luǒ	bare, nude, undress, strip
锵	qiāng	tinkle, clang, jingle	贾	jiǎ	surname, merchant, buy, trade	逗	dòu	tempt, allure, arouse, stir
寓	yù	residence, lodge, dwell	咚	dōng	used as description of sound	璞	pú	unpolished gem, uncarved gem
烫	tàng	scald, heat, wash, iron clothes	铅	qiān	lead plumbum	啸	xiào	roar, howl, scream, whistle
炳	bǐng	bright, luminous, glorious	屿	yǔ	island	竖	shù	vertical, perpendicular, upright
惶	huáng	fearful, afraid, anxious, nervous	仕	shì	official, serve government	挪	nuó	move, shift on one side
栅	zhà	fence, palisade, grid	迄	qì	extend, reach, until, till	顷	qǐng	a moment, to lean
窄	zhǎi	narrow, tight, narrow-minded	鸥	ōu	seagull, tern, Larus species (various)	鲢	lián	silver carp, hypophthalmiathys
郊	jiāo	suburbs, waste land, open spaces	倩	qiàn	beautiful, lovely, son-in-law	兜	dōu	pouch
茧	jiǎn	cocoon, callus, blister	磊	lěi	pile of rocks or stones, great	抒	shū	express, eliminate, relieve

夷	yí	ancient barbarian tribes	绰	chuò	graceful, delicate, spacious	溯	sù	go upstream, go against current, formerly
拙	zhuó	stupid, clumsy, crude, convention	僚	liáo	companion, colleague, officials, bureaucracy	芙	fú	hibiscus
杖	zhàng	cane, walking stick	溃	kuì	flooding river, militarily defeat	凶	xiōng	culprit, murder, bad, sad
鸽	gē	pigeon, dove, Columba species (various)	妒	dù	jealous, envious	沌	dùn	chaotic, confused, turbid, murky
祺	qí	good luck, good fortune	呐	nè	raise voice, yell out loud, shout, stammer	卦	guà	fortune telling, tell fortunes
聆	líng	listen, hear	栖	qī	perch, roost, stay	蝇	yíng	flies
佮	gé	(Cant.) intensive particle	唾	tuò	spit, spit on, saliva	汇	huì	collect, compile, assemble, hedgehog
楣	méi	crossbeam above or under gate	匠	jiàng	craftsman, artisan, workman	蛛	zhū	spider
悼	dào	grieve, mourn, lament, grieved	舜	shùn	legendary ruler	耿	gěng	bright, shining, have guts
瞄	miáo	take aim at, look at	芋	yù	taro	瞒	mán	deceive, lie, eyes half-closed
竭	jié	put forth great effort, exhaust	茵	yīn	a cushion, mattress, wormwood	吼	hǒu	roar, shout, bark, howl
苛	kē	small, petty, harsh, rigorous	浸	jìn	soak, immerse, dip, percolate	拯	zhěng	help, save, aid, lift, raise
克	kè	subdue, overcome, cut down	豆	dòu	beans, peas, bean-shaped	沛	pèi	abundant, full, copious, sudden
掠	lvè	rob, ransack, plunder, pass by	廊	láng	corridor, porch, veranda	凸	tū	protrude, bulge out, convex
搅	jiǎo	disturb, agitate, stir up	俺	ǎn	personal pronoun, I	酌	zhuó	serve wine, feast, deliberate
倡	chàng	guide, leader, lead, introduce	朦	méng	condition or appearance of moon	蕉	jiāo	banana, plantain

暱	nì — intimate, close, approach	焕	huàn — shining, brilliant, lustrous	掏	tāo — take out, pull out, clean out
蝉	chán — cicada, continuous	焰	yàn — flame, blaze, glowing, blazing	狄	dí — tribe from northern china, surnam
绳	shéng — rope, string, cord, measure, restrain	惰	duò — indolent, careless, lazy, idle	芽	yá — bud, sprout, shoot
裹	guǒ — wrap, bind, encircle, confine	宛	wǎn — seem, as if, crooked	御	yù — defend, resist, hold out against
赎	shú — buy, redeem, ransome, atone for	燥	zào — dry, parched, arid, quick-tempered	滔	tāo — overflow, rushing water, a torrent
贬	biǎn — decrease, lower, censure, criticize	悍	hàn — courageous, brave, violent	袂	mèi — sleeves
坟	fén — grave, mound, bulge, bulging	颉	jié — fly upward, soar, contest, to rob	啤	pí — beer
押	yā — mortgage, pledge, deposit, to pawn	尴	gān — embarrassed, ill at ease	颤	zhàn — shiver, tremble, trembling
钝	dùn — blunt, obtuse, dull, flat, dull-witted	腥	xīng — raw meat, rank, strong-smelling	缔	dì — tie, join, connect, connection
粮	liáng — food, grain, provisions	哑	yǎ — dumb, mute, become hoarse	槟	bīn — betelnut, areca nut
簿	bó — register, account book, notebook	斧	fǔ — axe, hatchet, chop, hew	肿	zhǒng — swell, swollen, swelling
纶	lún — green silk thread or tassel	僵	jiāng — stiff and motionless, stock still	龃	chū — act, stanza, time, occasion
辖	xiá — linchpin of wheel, control	蹲	dūn — squat, crouch, idle about	敷	fū — spread, diffuse, apply, paint
喘	chuǎn — pant, gasp, breathe heavily	酿	niàng — brew, ferment	佑	yòu — help, protect, bless
肖	xiào — look like, resemble, be like	愈	yù — more and more, even more	隧	suì — tunnel, underground passageway, path to a tomb
嗜	shì — be fond of, have weakness for	檬	méng — type of locust oracacia	迳	jìng — pass by, approach, direct

碌	lù	rough, uneven, rocky, mediocre
襟	jīn	lapel, collar
凋	diāo	be withered, fallen, exhausted
圭	guī	jade pointed at top
寇	kòu	bandits, thieves, enemy, invade
污	wū	filthy, dirty, impure, polluted
哨	shào	whistle, blow whistle, chirp
倪	ní	feeble, tiny, young and weak
筠	yún	bamboo skin, bamboo
桦	huà	type of birch
诈	zhà	cheat, defraud, swindle, trick, to feign
姜	jiāng	surname, ginger
旬	xún	ten-day period, period of time
秃	tū	bald, bare, stripped
脂	zhī	fat, grease, lard, grease
噢	yǔ	moan, interjection for pain, sad
撼	hàn	move, shake, (Cant.) to fight
衅	xìn	smear with blood in sacrifice, rift, quarrel
庚	gēng	7th heavenly stem
炫	xuàn	shine, glitter, show off, flaunt
谭	tán	surname, to talk
惭	cán	ashamed, humiliated, shameful
涩	sè	astringent, harsh, uneven, rough
崔	cuī	high, lofty, towering, surname
贷	dài	lend, borrow, pardon
胡	hú	beard, mustache, whiskers
晒	shài	dry in sun, expose to sun
琉	liú	sparkling stone, glazed, opaque
捏	niē	pick with fingers, knead, mold
绮	qǐ	fine thin silk, elegant, beautifu
膝	xī	knee
拭	shì	wipe away stains with cloth
暗	àn	dark, obscure, in secret, covert
醋	cù	vinegar, jealousy, envy
膨	péng	to swell, swollen, bloated, inflated
杠	gāng	lever, pole, crowbar, sharpen
鑫	xīn	used in names
瀑	pù	waterfall, cascade, heavy rain
喃	nán	keep talking, chattering, mumble
剖	pōu	split in two, slice, dissect
袜	wà	socks, stockings
逾	yú	go over, pass over, exceed
涅	niè	blacken, black mud, slime, tatto
扳	bān	pull, drag, right itself
惘	wǎng	disconcerted, dejected, discouraged
凳	dèng	bench, stool
呃	è	belch, hiccup
掘	jué	dig, excavate, excavate cave

捍	hàn	ward off, guard against, defend
蜗	guā	a snail, Eulota callizoma
暇	xiá	leisure, relaxation, spare time
抉	jué	choose, select, gouge, pluck out
钩	gōu	hook, barb, sickle, stroke with
匡	kuāng	correct, restore, revise
哔	bì	used in transliterations
谛	dì	careful, attentive
晦	huì	dark, unclear, obscure, night
傍	bàng	by side of, beside, near, close
堤	dī	dike
谍	dié	an intelligence report, to spy, spying
耸	sǒng	urge on, rise up, stir, excite, to raise up
忿	fèn	get angry, fury, exasperation
驴	lü	donkey, ass
绽	zhàn	ripped seam, rend, crack
榔	láng	betel-nut tree
旷	kuàng	extensive, wide, broad, empty
稻	dào	rice growing in field, rice plant
辗	zhǎn	turn over, roll
卜	bó	radish
蜘	zhī	spider
窟	kū	hole, cave, cellar, underground
溢	yì	overflow, brim over, full
伶	líng	lonely, solitary, actor
葱	cōng	scallions, onions, leeks
恍	huǎng	seemingly, absent-minded
禧	xī	happiness, congratulations
瀚	hàn	vast, wide, extensive
泓	hóng	clear, deep pool of water
罕	hǎn	rare, scarce, surname
刃	rèn	edged tool, cutlery, knife edge
窍	qiào	hole, opening, aperture
梵	fàn	Buddhist, Sanskrit
柠	níng	lemon
蔚	wèi	luxuriant, thick, ornamental
莺	yīng	oriole, green finch, Sylvia species (various)
祯	zhēn	lucky, auspicious, good omen
亟	jí	urgently, immediately, extremely
黛	dài	blacken eyebrows, black
逮	dài	seize, catch, reach, arrive
刁	diāo	tricky, sly, crafty, cunning
匣	xiá	small box, case, coffer
轿	jiào	sedan-chair, palanquin
斐	fěi	graceful, elegant, beautiful
拐	guǎi	kidnap, abduct, turn
沫	mò	froth, foam, bubbles, suds
窈	yǎo	obscure, secluded, refined

渝	yú	change, chongqing	仄	zè	slanting, oblique, oblique tones	瑛	yīng	luster of gem, crystal
葵	kuí	sunflower, measure	噜	lū	verbose, talkative, mumbling	绣	xiù	embroider, embroidery, ornament
奕	yì	in sequence, orderly, abundant	窥	kuī	peep, watch, spy on, pry	浏	liú	clear, bright, whistling
隶	lì	be subservient to, servant	蔽	bì	cover, hide, conceal, shelter	仟	qiān	one thousand, leader of one thousand men
敛	liàn	draw back, fold back, collect	丞	chéng	assist, aid, rescue	诘	jié	question, interrogate
鳖	biē	turtle	疤	bā	scar, cicatrix, birthmark	膏	gāo	grease, fat, paste, ointment
锥	zhuī	gimlet, awl, drill, auger, bore	窕	tiǎo	slender, quiet and modest, charming	皱	zhòu	wrinkles, creases, folds
晰	xī	clear, evident, clearly	晖	huī	sunshine, light, bright, radiant	舅	jiù	mother's brother, uncle
孰	shú	who? which? what? which one?	煽	shān	stir up, incite, agitate, provoke	姚	yáo	handsome, elegant, surname
钞	chāo	paper money, bank notes, copy	袱	fú	a piece of cloth used wrap bundles	绊	bàn	loop, catch, fetter, shackle
焚	fén	burn	芦	lú	rushes, reeds	咸	xián	salty, briny, salted, pickled
沮	jū	stop, prevent, defeated, dejected	呕	ōu	to vomit, annoy, enrage	瞪	dèng	stare at
淳	chún	honest, simple, unsophisticated, cyanogen	丐	gài	beggar, beg, give	茹	rú	roots, vegetables, eat, bear
盘	pán	tray, plate, dish, examine	菱	líng	water-chestnut, water caltrop	篠	xiǎo	dwarf bamboo, diminutive in person's name
涕	tì	tear, snivel, nasal mucus	衬	chèn	underwear, inner garments	蚀	shí	nibble away, erode, eclipse
溉	gài	water, irrigate, flood, wash	瑄	xuān	a ornamental piece of jade several inches across	翟	dí	surname, a kind of pheasant, plumes

怠 dài — idle, remiss, negligent, neglect	钰 yù — rare treasure	躯 qū — body
肺 fèi — lungs	掷 zhí — throw (down), hurl, cast, fling	丑 chǒu — ugly looking, homely, disgraceful
奢 shē — extravagant, wasteful, exaggerate	荫 yìn — shade, shelter, protect	靶 bǎ — target, splashboard on chariot
纱 shā — gauze, thin silk, yarn, thread	芸 yún — rue, an herb used keep insects away	佰 bǎi — hundred
峻 jùn — high, steep, towering, stern	阱 jǐng — pitfall, trap, snare	哄 hōng — coax, beguile, cheat, deceive
肾 shèn — kidneys, testes, gizzard	囡 nān — one's daughter, to filch, to secrete	阑 lán — door screen, railing fence
戳 chuō — prick, stab, stamp, seal, chop	腕 wàn — wrist	菸 yān — to fade, withered or dried leaves, tobacco
凹 āo — concave, hollow, depressed, a pass, valley	蟾 chán — toad	蒐 sōu — collect, gather, assemble, seek
呱 gū — wail, crying of child, swear at	巾 jīn — kerchief, towel, turban, KangXi radical number 50	雏 chú — chick, fledging, infant, toddler
螃 páng — crab	盯 chéng — rivet gaze upon, keep eyes on	馈 kuì — offer food superior, send gift
垄 lǒng — grave, mound, ridge in field	毓 yù — give birth to, bring up, educate	犀 xī — rhinoceros, sharp, well-tempered
逞 chěng — indulge oneself, brag, show off	姨 yí — mother/wife's sister, concubine	穆 mù — majestic, solemn, reverent, calm
樵 qiáo — woodcutter, firewood, gather wood	阀 fá — powerful and influential group	弥 mí — extensive, full, fill, complete
跷 qiāo — raise one's foot	搁 gē — place, put, lay down, delay	隙 xì — crack, split, fissure, grudge
疵 cī — flaw, fault, defect, disease	憧 chōng — irresolute, indecisive, yearn for	忏 chàn — regret, repent, confess sins
琨 kūn — beautiful jade, precious stones	阙 què — watch tower, palace	萱 xuān — day-lily, hemerocallisflava

怅	chàng disappointed, dissatisfied	辄	zhé sides of chariot where weapons	搏	bó seize, spring upon, strike
榕	róng banyan tree	饥	jī starve, be hungry, famine	捣	dǎo hull, thresh, beat, attack
渣	zhā refuse, dregs, lees, sediment	眺	tiào look at, gaze at, scan, survey	虞	yú concerned about, anxious, worried
俯	fǔ bow down, face down, look down	绅	shēn girdle, tie, bind, gentry	谤	bàng slander, libel
珑	lóng a gem cut like dragon	咫	zhǐ foot measure of Zhou dynasty	俏	qiào like, similar, resemble, pretty
淆	yáo confused, in disarray, mixed up	蜀	shǔ name of an ancient state	楠	nán name of tree, machilus nanmu
乞	qǐ beg, request	诅	zǔ curse, swear, pledge	匀	yún equal, impartially, uniform, even
貂	diāo marten, sable, mink	寰	huán great domain, country, world	诓	wàng travel, go to, deceive, scare
敞	chǎng roomy, spacious, open, broad	跪	guì kneel	囚	qiú prisoner, convict, confine
溺	nì drown, submerge in water, indulge	骆	luò a white horse with black mane, a camel	憬	jǐng rouse, awaken, become conscious
苇	wěi reed	脊	jí spine, backbone, ridge	瑶	yáo precious jade
疆	jiāng boundary, border, frontier	乍	zhà first time, for the first time	眸	móu pupil of eye, eye
窜	cuàn run away, revise, edit, expel	孽	niè evil, son of concubine, ghost	卅	sà thirty, thirtieth
夭	yǎo young, fresh-looking, die young	簧	huáng reed of woodwind instrument	徘	pái walk back and forth, hesitate
馒	mán steamed bread, steamed dumplings	趴	pā lying prone, leaning over	鎚	chuí hammer, mallet, club
啼	tí weep, whimper, howl, twitter	冗	rǒng excessive, superfluous	缉	qì to sew in close stitches

Character	Pinyin	Definition	Character	Pinyin	Definition	Character	Pinyin	Definition
絮	xù	waste cotton, raw silk or cotton	啄	zhuó	to peck, (Cant.) to slander	沸	fèi	boil, bubble up, gush
萃	cuì	dense, thick, close-set, to collect together	嘶	sī	neighing of a horse, gravel voiced, husky throated	鸳	yuān	male mandarin duck (Aix galericulata)
禽	qín	birds, fowl, surname,, capture	惫	bèi	tired, weary, fatigued	徨	huáng	doubtful, irresolute, vacillating
屐	jī	wooden shoes, clogs	輿	yú	cart, palanquin, public opinion	邂	xiè	unexpected meeting, encounter by
掀	xiān	lift, raise, stir	嫖	piào	patronize prostitutes, frequent	苟	gǒu	illicit, grammatical particle: if, but
台	tái	table	矫	jiǎo	correct, rectify, straighten out	铎	duó	bell, surname
棱	léng	squared timber, angle, edge	哗	huā	rushing sound, gush forward	徊	huái	linger, walk to and fro, hesitain
拱	gǒng	fold hands on breast, bow, salute	蕙	huì	species of fragrant orchid	徬	páng	to wander about, walk along side of
滞	zhì	block up, obstruct, stagnant	吠	fèi	bark	妞	niū	girl
氾	fàn	overflow, flood, inundate	芹	qín	celery	叩	kòu	knock, ask, kowtow, bow
朽	xiǔ	decayed, rotten, rot, decay	侪	chái	a company, companion, together	赦	shè	forgive, remit, pardon
汐	xì	night tides, evening ebb tide	虔	qián	act with reverence, reverent	茅	máo	reeds, rushes, grass, surname
棠	táng	crab apple tree, wild plums	仑	lún	logical reasons, logical order	膳	shàn	meals, provisions, board
魉	liǎng	a kind of monster	儡	lěi	puppet, dummy	鸯	yāng	female mandarin duck (Aix galericulata)
懦	nuò	weak, timid, cowardly	渗	shèn	soak through, infiltrate	邵	shào	surname, various place names
筱	xiǎo	dwarf bamboo, diminutive in person's name	畜	chù	livestock, domestic animals	崖	yá	cliff, precipice, precipitous

瑕	xiá	flaw in gem, fault, defect
擒	qín	catch, capture, seize, arrest
莽	mǎng	thicket, underbrush, poisonous
弧	hú	wooden bow, arc, crescent
奎	kuí	one of the twenty-eight lunar mansions
饵	ěr	bait, bait, entice, dumplings
蔓	màn	creeping plants, tendrils, vines
衔	xián	bit, hold in mouth, bite, gag
萎	wēi	wither, wilt
铸	zhù	melt, cast, coin, mint
壤	rǎng	soil, loam, earth, rich
恃	shì	rely on, presume on, trust to
汀	tīng	sandbar, beach, bank, shore
粥	zhōu	rice gruel, congee
脖	bó	neck
锻	duàn	forge metal, temper, refine
蕊	ruǐ	unopened flowers, flower buds
挂	guà	hang, suspend, suspense
矽	xì	silicon
澈	chè	thoroughly, completely
裘	qiú	fur garments, surname
偎	wēi	cling to, cuddle, embrace, fondle
彗	huì	broomstick, comet
苟	jì	to be circumspect, cautious in ones behaviour
廓	kuò	broad, wide, open, empty, to expand
茎	jīng	stem, stalk
浇	jiāo	spray, water, sprinkle
瞻	zhān	look, look out for, respect
椒	jiāo	pepper, spices
磅	bàng	pound, weigh
吨	dūn	metric ton
笙	shēng	small gourd-shaped musical instrument
揣	chuǎi	put things under clothes
屯	tún	village, hamlet, camp, station
侏	zhū	small, little, tiny, dwarf
饺	jiǎo	stuffed dumplings
塌	tā	fall in ruins, collapse
泻	xiè	drain off, leak, flow, pour down
樽	zūn	goblet, jar, jug, lush
磋	cuō	polish, buff, scrutinize
悯	mǐn	pity, sympathize with, grieve for
歼	jiān	annihilate, wipe out, kill off
蚤	zǎo	flea, louse
拼	pàn	risk, disregard, go all out for
嚼	jiáo	prattle, be glib
勘	kān	investigate, compare, collate
澜	lán	overflowing, waves, ripples
厄	è	adversity, difficulty, distress

嚷	rǎng	shout, brawl, make uproar, cry	伽	jiā	tample	徽	huī	a badge, insignia
隅	yú	corner, nook, remote place	寥	liáo	few, scarce, empty, deserted	缤	bīn	flourishing, thriving, abundant
帘	lián	a blind, screen, curtain	烘	hōng	bake, roast, dry by fire	茜	qiàn	madder, rubia cordifolia, reeds
驯	xún	tame, docile, obedient	噎	yē	choke, hiccup	厦	shà	big building, mansion
闰	rùn	intercalary, extra, surplus	煤	méi	coal, coke, charcoal, carbon	链	liàn	chain, wire, cable, chain, shack
锈	xiù	rust, corrode	诫	jiè	warn, admonish, warning	颊	jiá	cheeks, jaw
俐	lì	smooth, active, clever, sharp	曳	yì	trail, tow, drag, pull	蓓	bèi	bud
暧	ài	obscure, dim, ambiguous, vague	郤	xì	crack, opening, surname	淌	tǎng	trickle, flow down, drip
喀	kè	vomit, used in transliterations	昆	kūn	elder brother, descendants	蔑	miè	disdain, disregard, slight
峙	zhì	stand erect, stand up, pile up	躁	zào	tense, excited, irritable	菇	gū	mushrooms
逅	hòu	meet unexpectedly	雇	gù	employ, to hire	殴	ōu	beat, fight with fists, hit, to strike, brawl
泌	mì	to seep out, excrete	酥	sū	butter, flaky, crispy, light, fluffy	缮	shàn	repair, mend, rewrite, transcribe
莓	méi	moss, edible berries	辕	yuán	axle, magistrate's office, surname	骇	hài	terrify, frighten, scare, shock
巍	wēi	high, lofty, majestic, eminent	糗	qiǔ	parched wheat or rice, broken grain	扛	káng	carry on shoulders, lift
杏	xìng	apricot, almond	茁	zhuó	to sprout, flourish, vigorous	琵	pí	guitar-like instrument
礁	jiāo	reef, jetty, submerged rocks	秽	huì	dirty, unclean, immoral, obscene	岔	chà	diverge, branch off, fork in road

僻 pì	out-of-the-way, remote, unorthodox	焊 hàn	weld, solder	嗡 wēng	sound of flying bees, airplanes
诵 sòng	recite, chant, repeat	瞌 kē	doze off, sleepy	捌 bā	break open, split open
遁 dùn	hide, conceal oneself, escape	赃 zāng	booty, loot, stolen goods, bribe	涡 wō	swirl, whirlpool, eddy
琮 cóng	octagonal piece of jade with hole in middle	卯 mǎo	4th terrestrial branch, period from 5-7 a.m.	锯 jù	a saw, to saw, amputate
扔 rēng	throw, hurl, throw away, cast	苏 sū	revive, resurrect, a species of thyme	邹 zōu	name of an ancient state, surname
莅 lì	reach, arrive, manage	隘 ài	narrow, confined, a strategic pass	蹋 tà	step on, tread on, stumble, slip
湛 zhàn	deep, profound, clear, tranquil, placid	昼 zhòu	daytime, daylight	岫 xiù	mountain peak, cave, cavern
蛰 zhí	to hibernate	桩 zhuāng	stake, post, affair, matter	藐 miǎo	disregard, slight, disdain
汲 jí	draw water from well, imbibe	禄 lù	blessing, happiness, prosperity	皂 zào	soap, black, menial servant
濑 lài	swift current, rapids	绒 róng	silk, cotton, or woolen fabric	眈 dān	indulge in, be negligent
粪 fèn	manure, dung, night soil	粤 yuè	Guangdong and Guangxi provinces, initial particle	卤 lǔ	saline soil, natural salt, rock
曜 yào	glorious, as sun, daylight, sunlight	懋 mào	splendid, grand, majestic	咎 jiù	fault, defect, error, mistake
痘 dòu	smallpox	聂 niè	whisper, surname	垢 gòu	dirt, filth, stains, dirty
瞳 tóng	pupil of eye	闵 mǐn	mourn, grieve, urge on, incite	睿 ruì	shrewd, astute, clever, keen
跤 jiāo	stumble, fall down, wrestle	躬 gōng	body, personally, in person	斟 zhēn	to pour wine or tea into a cup, to gauge
淇 qí	river in Henan province	苣 jǔ	hemp-like plant, taro, herb	毯 tǎn	rug, carpet, blanket

幸	xìng	luck(ily), favor, fortunately	骋	chěng	gallop horse, hasten, hurry	岱	dài	Daishan, one of the Five Sacred Mountains in China
庐	lú	hut, cottage, name of a mountain	殃	yāng	misfortune, disaster, calamity	橄	gǎn	olive
恤	xù	show pity, relieve, help	叽	jī	sigh in disapproval, take small	鳞	lín	fish scales
蒙	méng	cover, ignorant, suffer, mongolia	芥	jiè	mustard plant, mustard, tiny	榄	lǎn	olive
楷	kǎi	model style of Chinese writing	硫	liú	sulfur	苔	tái	moss, lichen
麒	qí	legendary auspicious animal	椎	zhuī	hammer, mallet, vertebra	禹	yǔ	legendary hsia dynasty founder
喙	huì	beak, bill, snout, pant	厘	lí	manage, control, 1/1000 of a foot	袅	niǎo	curling upwards, wavering gently
亥	hài	12th terrestrial branch	倌	guān	assistant in wine shop, groom	吭	háng	throat
诃	hē	scold loudly, curse, abuse	裔	yì	progeny, descendants, posterity	梓	zǐ	catalpa ovata
蓦	mò	suddenly, quickly, abruptly	岩	yán	cliff, rocks, mountain	帜	zhì	flag, pennant, sign, fasten
瓣	bàn	petal, segment, valves	狡	jiǎo	cunning, deceitful, treacherous	惕	tì	be cautious, careful, alert
怯	qiè	lacking in courage, afraid	嫩	nèn	soft, tender, delicate, young	龚	gōng	give, present, reverential
嚎	háo	cry loudly, yell, scream	豚	tún	small pig, suckling pig, suffle	埠	bù	port city
暸	liáo	bright, clear	唆	suō	make mischief, incite, instigate	妃	fēi	wife, spouse, imperial concubine
瓢	piáo	ladle made from dried gourd	蹄	tí	hoof, leg of pork, little witch	厮	sī	servant
讥	jī	ridicule, jeer, mock, inspect	啃	kěn	gnaw, chew, bite	琶	pá	guitar-like instrument

愿	yuàn	desire, want, wish, ambition	噱	jué	laugh heartily, laugh aloud	狷	juàn	rash, impetuous, impulsive
搪	táng	ward off, evade, parry, block	氢	qīng	amonia, hydrogen nitride	橙	chéng	orange
咆	páo	roar	靡	mǐ	divide, disperse, scatter	砌	qì	stone steps, brick walk
筷	kuài	chopsticks	兑	duì	cash, exchange, barter, weight	湿	shī	damp, moist, dampness, moisture
呸	pēi	expression of reprimand	镀	dù	plate, coat, gild	踹	chuài	trample, tread on, kick, to crush
冢	zhǒng	burial mound, mausoleum, grand	祟	suì	evil spirit, evil influence	懈	xiè	idle, relaxed, remiss
术	shù	art, skill, special feat, method, technique	搓	cuō	to rub or roll between the hands	攸	yōu	distant, far, adverbial prefix
橡	xiàng	chestnut oak, rubber tree, rubber	膛	táng	chest, hollow space, cavity	俞	yú	surname, consent, approve
祉	zhǐ	happiness, blessings, good luck	冀	jì	hope for, wish, Hebei province	炊	chuī	cook, meal
瓷	cí	crockery, porcelain, chinaware	遐	xiá	afar, distant, old, advanced in	揽	lǎn	grasp, take hold of, monopolize
鹭	lù	heron, egret, Ardea species (various)	茄	qié	eggplant	蜢	měng	grasshopper
塘	táng	pond, tank, dike, embankment	郡	jùn	administrative division	韬	tāo	sheath, scabbard, bow case
挟	xié	clasp under arm, hold to bosom	牟	móu	make, seek, get, barley, low	糙	cāo	coarse, harsh, rough, unpolished rice
阎	yán	village gate, surname	旻	mín	heaven	赘	zhuì	unnecessary, superfluous
霆	tíng	a sudden peal of thunder	呎	chǐ	foot	炭	tàn	charcoal, coal, carbon
霄	xiāo	sky, clouds, mist, night	媳	xí	daughter-in-law	瘤	liú	tumor, lump, goiter

猿	yuán — ape	飏	yáng — soar, fly, float, scatter	铠	kǎi — armor, chain mail
蝠	fú — kind of bat	钜	jù — steel, iron, great	苓	líng — fungus, tuber, licorice
傀	guī — great, gigantic, puppet	烬	jìn — cinders, ashes, embers, remnants	墅	shù — villa, country house
璇	xuán — beautiful jade, star	困	kùn — be tired, sleepy	愣	léng — be in a daze
恬	tián — quiet, calm, tranquil, peaceful	嫉	jí — jealousy, be jealous of	琐	suǒ — fragments, trifling, petty, troublesome
嫂	sǎo — sister-in-law, elder brother's wife	淼	miǎo — a wide expanse of water	梳	shū — comb, brush
憎	zēng — hate, detest, abhor, hatred	搂	lǒu — hug, embrace, drag, pull	藻	zǎo — splendid, magnificent, algae
酵	xiào — yeast, leaven	屉	tì — drawer, tray, pad, screen	陡	dǒu — steep, sloping, abruptly, sudden
摺	zhé — fold, bend, twisted, curved	箫	xiāo — musical instrument like pan-pipes, bamboo flute	饷	xiǎng — host banquet, banquet
桐	tóng — name applied various trees	蚱	zhà — grasshopper, (edible) locust, cicada	曦	xī — sunlight, sunshine, early dawn
璧	bì — piece of jade with hole in it	偈	jié — brave, martial, hasty, scudding	蹦	bèng — hop, leap, jump, bright
昶	chǎng — a long day. bright. extended. clear	咙	lóng — throat	铮	zhēng — clanging sound, small gong
嗤	chī — laugh at, ridicule, sneer, snort	戌	xū — 11th terrestrial branch	耘	yún — weed
裳	cháng — clothes, skirt, beautiful	啾	jiū — wailing of child, chirp	嵘	róng — high, steep, lofty, towering
胺	è — amine	笃	dǔ — deep, true, sincere, genuine	烹	pēng — boil, cook, quick fry, stir fry
巩	gǒng — bind, firm, secure, strong	厝	cuò — cut or engrave, a grave or tombstone	疚	jiù — chronic disease, chronic illness, sorrow

鸶	sī	egret, Egretta garzetta	洶	xiōng	the rush of water, turbulent, noisy, restless	薔	qiáng	rose
沐	mù	bathe, cleanse, wash, shampoo	咽	yān	throat, pharynx	烙	luò	brand, burn, branding iron
畸	jī	odd, fractional, remainder, odds	讳	huì	conceal, shun, regard as taboo	揍	zòu	hit, beat, smash, break
曙	shù	bright, light of rising sun	铐	kào	shackles, manacle	朔	shuò	first day of lunar month, the north
涓	juān	brook, stream, select, pure	睬	cǎi	notice, pay attention to	矶	jī	jetty, submerged rock, eddy
岐	qí	high, majestic, fork in road	凄	qī	bitter cold, miserable, dreary	鲫	jì	carassius auratus, crucian carp
楞	léng	used for Ceylon in Buddhist texts	鲤	lǐ	carp	荆	jīng	thorns, brambles, my wife, cane
偕	xié	together, be in order	徜	cháng	walking and fro, lingering	饥	jī	starve, be hungry, famine
肮	āng	dirty	蔼	ǎi	lush, affable, friendly	辙	chè	wagon ruts, wheel tracks
恁	rèn	that, like this, thus, so, such	霈	pèi	torrential rains, flow of water	诛	zhū	execute, kill, put to death, punish
鞠	jú	bow, bend, rear, raise, nourish	茉	mò	white jasmine	煜	yù	bright, shining, brilliant
佣	yōng	hire, employ, charter, servant	嗓	sǎng	voice, throat	酹	lèi	to pour out a libation, to sprinkle
昙	tán	become cloudy, overcast	铨	quán	weigh, measure, select officials	艳	yàn	beautiful, sexy, voluptuous
绷	bēng	bind, draw firmly, strap	峨	é	lofty	揉	róu	rub, massage, crush by hand
珈	jiā	an ornament attached to a woman's hairpin	鹃	juān	cuckoo	诲	huì	teach, instruct, encourage, urge
臆	yì	chest, breast, bosom, thought	隽	jùn	superior, outstanding, talented	熔	róng	melt, smelt, fuse, mold

堇	jǐn	yellow loam, clay, season, few	韧	rèn	strong and pliable, resilient	扒	bā	scratch, dig up, crawl, crouch
憨	hān	foolish, silly, coquettish	舵	duò	rudder, helm	肛	gāng	anus
戊	wù	5th heavenly stem	坝	bà	embankment, dam	抠	kōu	raise, lift up, tight-fisted
骷	kū	skeleton	碘	diǎn	iodine	鞍	ān	saddle, any saddle-shaped object
冕	miǎn	crown, ceremonial cap	榨	zhà	to press or extract juices	肘	zhǒu	the elbow, help a person shoulder a load
羔	gāo	lamb, kid	哺	bǔ	chew food, feed	霓	ní	rainbow, variegated, colored
巳	sì	the hours from 9 to 11, 6th terrestrial branch	铲	chǎn	spade, shovel, trowel, scoop	蚵	hé	oyster
惆	chóu	distressed, regretful, sad	驹	jū	colt, fleet, swift, sun, surname	撷	xié	pick up, gather up, hold in lap
稽	jī	examine, investigate, delay	羹	gēng	soup, broth	纺	fǎng	spin, reel, weave, reeled pongee
蜕	shuì	molt, exuviate, shed	趾	zhǐ	toe, tracks, footprints	吊	diào	condole, mourn, pity, hang
豁	huò	open up, clear, exempt	褪	tùn	strip, undress, fall off, fade	癸	guǐ	10th heavenly stem
眨	zhǎ	wink	臻	zhēn	reach, arrive, utmost, superior	慷	kāng	ardent, generous, magnanimous
蝙	biān	bat	胧	lóng	condition or appearance of moon	沼	zhǎo	lake, fishpond, swamps
舱	cāng	hold of ship, cabin	柚	yòu	pomelo, grapefruit	抨	pēng	impeach, censure, attack
葭	jiā	bulrush, reed, flute, whistle	枷	jiā	cangue scaffold	靥	yè	dimples
硝	xiāo	saltpeter, niter, > to tan	绚	xuàn	variegated, adorned, brilliant	绞	jiǎo	twist, wring, intertwine, winch

缆	làn — hawser, heavy-duty rope, cable	讪	shàn — abuse, slander, vilify, ridicule	褚	chǔ — bag, valise, stuff, pad, surname
砗	chē — giant clam, tridacna gigas	嫣	yān — charming, fascinating, gay	蒲	pú — type of rush, vine
丫	yā — forked, bifurcation	鹦	yīng — parrot	蒹	jiān — reed, phragmites communis
憩	qì — rest, take rest	懊	ào — vexed, worried, nervous, regret	聋	lóng — deaf
盎	àng — cup, pot, bowl, abundant	婊	biǎo — whore, prostitute	盔	kuī — helmet, bowl, basin
峦	luán — mountain range, pointed mountain	矜	jīn — pity, feel sorry for, show sympat	凛	lǐn — shiver with cold or fear, fearful
鹉	wǔ — species of parrot	蜴	yì — lizard	惚	bū — absent-minded, confused
畴	chóu — farmland, arable land, category	羁	jī — halter, restrain, hold, control	媛	yuàn — beauty, beautiful woman
堑	qiàn — moat, trench, pit, cavity	疮	chuāng — tumor, boil, sore, wound	韶	sháo — music of the emperor Shun, beautiful
憋	biē — to suppress inner feelings, hasty	祁	qí — pray, numerous, ample, abundant	诟	gòu — abuse, scold, berate, insult
搔	sāo — to scratch	蜥	xī — lizard	袒	tǎn — strip, lay bare, bared, naked
奄	yǎn — ere long, remain, tarry, feeble	忱	chén — truth, sincerity, sincere	玖	jiǔ — black-colored jade
拌	bàn — mix	悴	cuì — suffer, become emaciated, haggard	祠	cí — ancestral temple, offer sacrifice
扼	è — grasp, clutch, choke, strangle	髅	lóu — skull, skeleton	筑	zhú — build, erect, building
蛤	há — clam	茱	zhū — dogwood	骐	qí — piebald horse, excellent horse
捶	chuí — strike with stick, lash, beat	须	xū — beard, whiskers, whisker-like	亢	kàng — high, proud, violent, excessive, skilled, name

艸	cǎo	grass, KangXi radical 140	筛	shāi	sieve, filter, screen, sift	岳	yuè	mountain peak, surname
岳	yuè	mountain peak, surname	慵	yōng	indolent, easy-going, lazy	戮	lù	kill, massacre, oppress
跎	tuó	slip, stumble, falter, vacillate	砰	pēng	sound of crashing stones, bang!	炜	wěi	brilliant red, glowing
篱	lí	bamboo or wooden fence, hedge	笈	jí	bamboo box used carry books	瘫	tān	paralysis, palsy, numbness
吏	lì	government official, magistrate	痊	quán	be healed, be cured, recover	庶	shù	numerous, various, multitude
厥	jué	personal pronoun he, she, it	棘	jí	jujube tree, thorns, brambles	娑	suō	dance, frolic, lounge, saunter
沁	qìn	soak into, seep in, percolate	窘	jiǒng	embarrassed, hard-pressed	鲸	jīng	whale
缕	lǚ	thread, detailed, precise	碱	jiǎn	alkaline, alkali, lye, salt	俨	yǎn	grave, respectful, majestic
栈	zhàn	warehouse, tavern, inn	蔬	shū	vegetables, greens	鸠	jiū	pigeon, dove, collect, assemble
闲	xián	fence, barrier, defend, idle time	迢	tiáo	far, distant	恣	zì	indulge oneself, unrestrained
昀	yún	sun light, used in personal names	泠	líng	nice and cool, mild and comfortable	涟	lián	flowing water, ripples, weeping
眩	xuàn	to confuse, dizzy, dazed, disoriented	噫	yī	belch, alas	娥	é	be beautiful, good, surname
荼	tú	bitter vegetable	鳄	è	crocodile, alligator	镖	biāo	dart, spear, harpoon, escort
侃	kǎn	upright and strong, amiable	虏	lǔ	to capture, imprison, seize, a prison	俾	bǐ	so that, in order that, cause
樟	zhāng	camphor tree	榴	liú	pomegranate	叮	níng	enjoin, instruct, charge
炬	jù	torch	窦	dòu	surname, hole, burrow, corrupt	笠	lì	bamboo hat, bamboo covering

翱	áo	soar, roam	莘	xīn	long, numerous, a marsh plant	蹰	chú	hesitate, falter, be undecided
翡	fěi	kingfisher, emerald, jade	姜	jiāng	surname, ginger	枭	xiāo	owl thus, something evil
匕	bǐ	spoon, ladle, knife, dirk	藩	fán	fence, boundary, outlying border	徉	yáng	wonder, rove, stray, hesitating
觴	shāng	wine vessel, propose toast, feast	拣	jiǎn	choose, select, pick up, gather	吱	zhī	chirping, squeaking, hissing
䀹	guī	follow, comply with	墉	yōng	wall, fortified wall, small wall	傌	mà	to curse, to revile, to abuse, to scold
梢	shāo	pointed tip of something long like a branch	巅	diān	summit of mountain, mountain top	踌	chóu	hesitate, falter, smug, self-satisfied
萌	méng	bud, sprout	幌	huǎng	curtain, cloth screen	杭	háng	cross stream, navigate
佼	jiǎo	be lucky, by chance, by luck	栾	luán	name of tree, a part of cornice	奠	diàn	pay respect, settle
痲	má	pock-marked, leprosy, measles	瘖	yīn	dumb, mute, unable speak	芯	xīn	pith from rush (juncus effusus)
蟀	shuài	cricket	驿	yì	relay station	耨	nòu	hoe, rake, weed
禾	hé	grain still on stalk, rice plant	瑾	jǐn	brilliance of gems, fine jade	塾	shú	village school, private tutorage
俭	jiǎn	temperate, frugal, economical	沱	tuó	rivers, streams, waterways, flow	腺	xiàn	gland
橱	chú	cabinet, wardrobe, cupboard	僵	jiāng	stiff and motionless, stock still	惋	wǎn	regret, be sorry, alarmed
擞	sǒu	shake, tremble, quake, flutter	噗	pū	burst	呛	qiāng	choke by smoke, irritates nose
蛀	zhù	insects that eat books, clothes	渲	xuàn	add repeated washes of color	酋	qiú	chief of tribe, chieftain
跆	tái	trample	塲	yì	a border, a limit, a dike, a frontier, a boundary	嬉	xī	enjoy, play, amuse oneself

怆	chuàng — sad, broken-hearted, disconsolate	噶	gé — used in transliterations	耙	pá — rake
憔	qiáo — be worn-out, emaciated, haggard	挠	náo — scratch, disturb, bother, submit	羲	xī — ancient emperor, breath, vapor
扑	pū — pound, beat, strike, attack	眶	kuàng — eye socket, rim of eye	蛎	lì — oyster
蹉	cuō — error, mistake, slip, failure	孵	fū — sit on eggs, hatch	淀	diàn — sediment, dregs, precipitate
恸	tòng — sadness, grief, mourn, be moved	灸	jiǔ — cauterize with moxa, moxibustion	愕	è — startled, alarmed, astonished
淤	yū — mud, sediment, clog up, silt up	狙	jū — an ape, monkey, to spy, watch for, to lie	槛	jiàn — threshold, door-sill
噢	yōng — oh	霎	shà — light rain, drizzle, an instant, passing	嗽	sòu — cough, gargle, clear throat
兢	jīng — fearful, cautious, wary	瑚	hú — coral, person of virtue	冉	rǎn — tender, weak, proceed gradually
甸	diàn — suburbs of capital, govern, crops	怔	zhēng — a disease resembling neurosis	蠹	dù — moth, insects which eat into clot
缀	zhuì — patch together, link, connect	谄	chǎn — flatter, truckle, toady	灼	zhuó — burn, broil, cauterize, bright
紊	wèn — confused, disorder	彤	tóng — red, vermilion, name of ancient	荐	jiàn — offer, present, recommend
诣	yì — reach, achievement, accomplishment	昧	mèi — dim, dark, obscure, blind	禀	bǐng — report to, petition
馏	liù — distill, distillation	蒜	suàn — garlic	窑	yáo — kiln, coal mine pit
讦	jié — expose other's secrets, pry	机	jī — machine, moment, chance	炯	jiǒng — bright, brilliant, clear, hot
颐	yí — cheeks, jaw, chin, rear, to nourish	缪	móu — wind around, bind, prepare	扉	fēi — door panel
嵩	sōng — high, lofty, one of the 5 peaks, situated in Hunan	缅	miǎn — distant, remote, think of	朕	zhèn — pronoun 'I'

蟋 xī cricket	濒 bīn approach, be on verge of, near	剔 tī pick out, scrape off, scrape meat
局 jú bureau, office, circumstance	钍 tǔ thorium	肋 lè ribs, chest
噩 è bad, ill-omened, unlucky	佢 qú he (Cant.)	揖 yī salute, bow, defer to, yield
圳 zhèn furrow in field, small drainage	芜 wú luxurious growth of weeds	亵 xiè dirty, ragged, slight, insult
嶄 zhǎn high, steep, precipitous, new	蜻 qīng dragonfly	坞 wù entrenchment, bank, low wall
绫 líng thin silk, damask silk	冶 yě smelt, fuse metals, cast, found	惦 diàn think of, remember, miss
梧 wú Sterculia platanifolia	罣 guà hinder, disturb, obstruct	殆 dài dangerous, perilous, endanger
兀 wù to cut off the feet	讼 sòng accuse, argue, dispute, litigate	臼 jiù mortar, bone joint socket
踮 diǎn tip toe	炙 zhì roast, broil, toast, cauterize	雌 cí female, feminine, gentle, soft
啧 zé interjection of approval or admiration	褒 bāo praise, commend, honor, cite	竺 zhú India, bamboo, surname
匈 xiōng breast, chest, thorax, clamor	葳 wēi luxuriant, flourishing, used for various plants	旱 hàn drought, dry, dry land
骰 tóu die, dice	阉 yān castrate, eunuch	甭 béng there is no need
欣 xīn happy, joyous, delighted	霏 fēi falling of snow and rain	酪 luò cream, cheese, koumiss
雍 yōng harmony, union, harmonious	饪 rèn cooked food, cook until well done	勋 xūn meritorious deed, merits, rank
煦 xǔ kind, gentle, gracious, genial	漓 lí short name for Guangxi province	娴 xián elegant, refined, skillful
揪 jiū grasp with hand, pinch	囝 jiǎn baby, infant	婵 chán beautiful, lovely, pretty, graceful

佼	jiǎo	beautiful, handsome, good-looking	玟	wén	streaks in jade, gem	荤	hūn	meat diet, strong smelling
俘	fú	prisoner of war, take as prisoner	癖	pǐ	craving, weakness for, indigestion	瞋	chēn	glare with anger
咄	duō	noise of rage, cry out in anger	幢	chuáng	carriage curtain, sun screen	迂	yū	doctrinaire, abstruse, unrealistic
蓊	wěng	luxuriant vegetation, lush	疹	zhěn	measles, rash, fever	儸	luó	bandit, daredevil
桔	jié	Chinese bellflower, well-swept	讹	é	swindle, cheat, erroneous, wrong	籐	téng	climbing plants, vines, cane
眯	mǐ	be blinded	猖	chāng	mad, wild, reckless, unruly	泄	xiè	leak, vent, flow, reveal
凿	záo	chisel, bore, pierce	咻	xiū	shout	晏	yàn	peaceful, quiet, clear, late in the day
诬	wú	make false accusation, defame	漪	yī	ripples on water, swirling	辫	biàn	braid, pigtail, plait, queue
蔺	lìn	rush used in making mats, surname	症	zhēng	obstruction of bowels	妾	qiè	concubine
琇	xiù	coarse variety of jasper or jade	蜓	tíng	dragonfly	烽	fēng	signal fire, tower where signal
舔	tiǎn	lick with tongue, taste	娣	dì	younger sister, sister-in-law	汶	wèn	a river in Shandong province
诏	zhào	decree, proclaim, imperial decree	侈	chǐ	luxurious, extravagant	膺	yīng	breast, chest, undertake, bear
渚	zhǔ	small sand bank, islet	槌	chuí	hammer, mallet, strike, beat	鞘	qiào	scabbard, sheath
噬	shì	bite, gnaw, snap at	咐	fù	instruct, order	璀	cuǐ	lustre of gems, glitter, shine
肪	fáng	animal fat	羚	líng	species of antelope	羿	yì	legendary archer
葫	hú	bottle-gourd	箔	bó	reed screen, frame for growing silkworms	庇	bì	cover, shield, shelter, protect

俪	lì — spouse, couple, pair	嘱	zhǔ — order, tell, instruct, leave word	颅	lú — skull
玺	xǐ — imperial signet, royal signet	褐	hé — coarse woolen cloth, dull, dark	擂	léi — rub, grind, grind with a mortar and pestle
遑	huáng — leisure, leisurely, hurry about	萦	yíng — entangle, entwine, coil	罹	lí — sorrow, grief, incur, meet with
粘	nián — viscous, mucous, glutinous	栗	lì — shiver, shudder, tremble, tremble	钊	zhāo — endeavor, strive, encourage, cut
彪	biāo — tiger, tiger stripes, tiger-like	瘀	yū — a hematoma, contusion, extravasted blood	蛾	é — moth
馁	něi — hungry, starving, famished	洹	huán — river in Henan province	谕	yù — proclaim, instruct, edict
胚	pēi — embryo, unfinished things	卉	huì — general term for plants, myriads	拇	mǔ — thumb, big toe
炽	chì — burning-hot, intense, to burn, blaze, splendid	睦	mù — friendly, amiable, peaceful	鲨	shā — shark
碴	chá — chipped edge of a container	辟	pì — law, rule, open up, develop	漱	shù — gargle, rinse, wash, scour
窒	zhì — stop up, obstruct	惺	xīng — intelligent, clever, astute	谲	jué — cunning, crafty, sly, wily
勦	jiǎo — destroy, exterminate, annihilate	迺	nǎi — then, thereupon, only then	臀	tún — buttocks
瘓	huàn — paralysis, numbness of limbs	渠	qú — ditch, canal, channel, gutter	弋	yì — catch, arrest, shoot with bow
狸	lí — fox	吽	óu — dull, stupid	痔	zhì — hemorrhoids, piles
霭	ǎi — cloudy sky, haze, calm, peaceful	轼	shì — horizontal wooden bar in front of a sedan chair	姥	mǔ — maternal grandmother, midwife
钙	gài — calcium	漾	yàng — overflow, swirl, ripple, to be tosssed by waves	跛	bǒ — lame
翎	líng — feather, plume, wing	磷	lìn — phosphorus, water rushing between	嗳	ài — interjection, exclamation

吩	fēn	order, command, instruct
鲍	bào	abalone, dried fish, surname
尩	wāng	lame
裴	péi	surname, look of a flowing gown
瞥	piē	take fleeting glance at
仝	tóng	together, same, surname
钳	qián	pincers, pliers, tongs
漩	xuán	eddy, whirlpool
荻	dí	reed, miscanthus sacchariflorus
茗	mǐng	tea, tea plant
椏	yā	the forking branch of a tree
靴	xuē	boots
矗	chù	straight, upright, erect, lofty
籽	zǐ	seed, pip, pit, stone
弩	nǔ	cross-bow, bow, downward stroke
翊	yì	flying, assist, help, respect
敕	chì	an imperial order or decree
俟	sì	wait for, wait until, as soon as
谚	yàn	proverb, maxim
汞	gǒng	element mercury
氯	lǜ	chlorine
瀛	yíng	sea, ocean
镕	róng	fuse, melt, smelt, mold
攘	ráng	seize, take by force, repel
咯	gē	final particle
桓	huán	variety of tree, surname
珀	pò	amber
咀	jǔ	suck, chew, masticate
瘴	zhàng	malaria pestilential vapors
晒	shài	dry in sun, expose to sun
洸	guāng	sparkle, glitter
背	bèi	back, back side, behind, betray
氙	dàn	xenon
婿	xù	son-in-law, husband
恺	kǎi	enjoy, be contented, joyful
剿	jiǎo	destroy, exterminate, annihilate
桨	jiǎng	oar, paddle
骸	hái	skeleton, body, leg bone
靓	jìng	make up face, ornament, quiet, (Cant.) pretty
垣	yuán	low wall
篑	kuì	a bamboo basket for carrying earth
浒	hǔ	riverbank, shore
痠	suān	aching of limbs, muscular pains
谷	gǔ	corn, grain, cereal, lucky
璟	jǐng	luster of gem
沥	lì	trickle, drip, strain, dregs
婪	lán	covet, covetous, avaricious
俑	yǒng	wooden figure buried with dead

磕	kē	hit, collide, knock into, sound
崝	zhēng	high, lofty, noble, steep, perilous
寐	mèi	sleep, be asleep
濯	zhuó	wash out, rinse, cleanse
陨	yǔn	fall, slip, let fall, die
鹂	lí	Chinese oriole, Oriolus oriolus
竑	hóng	be vast and endless, broad
阕	què	close, shut, watch tower
蚓	yǐn	earthworm
榷	què	footbridge, toll, levy, monopoly
夙	sù	early in morning, dawn, previous
谩	mán	deceive, insult
鳗	mán	eel
垚	yáo	mound, roundish mass
鸵	tuó	ostrich, Struthio camelus
墟	xū	high mound, hilly countryside, wasteland
暐	wěi	the bright shining of the sun
鹊	què	magpie, Pica species (various)
徙	xǐ	move one's abode, shift, migrate
堉	yù	ground, fertile land
丕	pī	great, grand, glorious, distinguished
笋	sǔn	bamboo shoot, joint, tendon
绎	yì	to unravel or unreel silk, to interpret, explain
燿	yào	shine, dazzle, brilliant, radiant
嗔	tián	be angry at, scold, rebuke
尸	shī	corpse, carcass
睐	lài	squint at, sidelong glance
璜	huáng	a semicircular jade ornament used as a pendant
棕	zōng	hemp palm, palm tree
蛊	gǔ	poison, venom, harm, bewitch
痹	bì	paralysis, numbness
旄	máo	a kind of ancient flag, old
撩	liáo	lift up, raise, leave, depart
昕	xīn	dawn, early morning, day
遴	lín	select, choose, surname
跋	bá	go by foot, epilogue, colophon
簇	cù	swarm, crowd together, cluster
鬓	bìn	hair on temples
镍	niè	nickel
胥	xū	all, together, mutually
嬴	yíng	to win, to have a surplus, surname
蜍	chú	toad
蚯	qiū	earthworm
湄	méi	water's edge, shore, bank
笺	jiān	note, memo, stationery, comments
讷	nè	slow of speech, mumble, stammer
殉	xùn	die for cause, be martyr for
檀	tán	sandalwood, hardwood, surname

竣	jùn — terminate, end, finish, quit	熹	xī — dim light, glimmer, warm, bright	沂	yí — river in southeast Shandong
峭	qiào — steep, precipitous, rugged	蒽	yuān — (Cant.) a bad smell	拈	nián — pick up with fingers, draw lots
隍	huáng — dry ditch, dry moat	鞑	dá — tatars	嗅	xiù — smell, scent, sniff, olfactive
佯	yáng — pretend, feign, false, deceitful	蚣	gōng — centipede	躏	lìn — trample down, oppress, overrun
雇	gù — employ, to hire	乩	jī — to divine	麓	lù — foot of hill, foothill
酗	xù — to become violent under the influence of alcohol	寅	yín — to respect, reverence, respectfully	洒	sǎ — sprinkle, splash, scatter, throw
媲	pì — marry off, pair, match, compare	瞩	zhǔ — watch carefully, stare at, focus on	钡	bèi — barium
诽	fěi — slander, vilify, condemn	拗	ǎo — to pull, drag, break off, to pluck (a flower)	朴	pú — simple, honest, plain, rough
罔	wǎng — net, deceive, libel, negative	螳	táng — mantis	撮	cuō — little bit, small amount, pinch
睽	kuí — staring	渍	zì — soak, steep, dye, stains, sodden	摹	mó — trace, copy, duplicate, pattern
扪	mén — stoke, pat, feel by hand, grope	搧	shān — fan, strike on face, stir up	蹂	róu — trample under foot, tread on
纾	shū — loosen, relax, relieve, extricate	蔗	zhè — sugar cane	晔	yè — bright, radiant, thriving
隼	zhǔn — aquiline (nose), a falcon	惮	dàn — dread, shrink from, shirk, fear	箍	gū — hoop, bind, surround
奚	xī — where? what? how? why?, servant	掳	lǔ — capture, seize	咿	yī — descriptive of creaking, laugh
渎	dú — ditch, sluice, gutter, drain	霾	mái — misty, foggy, dust storm	叨	tāo — talkative, quarrelous
邃	suì — profound, detailed, deep	稠	chóu — dense, crowded, packed, soupy	淮	huái — river in Anhui province

骁	xiāo — excellent horse, brave, valiant	咩	miē — the bleating of sheep	岑	cén — steep, precipitous, peak
聿	yù — writing brush, pencil, thereupon	吮	shǔn — suck with mouth, sip, lick	铳	chòng — ancient weapon, blunderbuss
癫	diān — crazy, mad, madness, mania, insanity	敖	áo — ramble, play about, leisurely	蜈	wú — centipede
钣	bǎn — plate	滂	pāng — torrential, voluminous	酉	yǒu — 10th terrestrial branch, a wine vessel
刍	chú — mow, cut grass, hay, fodder	谙	ān — versed in, fully acquainted with	虱	shī — louse, bug, parasite
坷	kě — clod of earth, lump of soil	笆	bā — bamboo fence	竽	yú — ancient woodwind instrument
椇	bèi — a palm-tree	賏	yìng — pearls or shells strung together	闺	guī — small entrance, women's quarters
浙	zhè — Zhejiang province, river	疙	gē — pimple, sore, boil, wart, pustule	蓁	zhēn — abundant, luxuriant vegetation
烷	wán — alkane	喈	jiē — music, melody	踤	zhuǎi — to waddle, to limp
酣	hān — enjoy intoxicants	卍	wàn — swastika fourth of auspicious	遏	è — stop, suppress, curb, check, a bar
亘	gèn — extend across, through, from	赑	bì — strong	万	wàn — ten thousand, innumerable
掐	qiā — hold, gather with hand, choke	蛹	yǒng — chrysalis, larva	骥	jì — thoroughbred horse, refined and
樊	fán — a railing, a fence an enclosed place	雱	páng — snowing heavily	戾	lì — perverse, recalcitrant, rebellious
别	bié — separate, other, do not	匮	guì — to lack	崛	jué — towering, eminent, rise abruptly
咨	zī — inquire, consult, discuss, plan	湃	pài — sound of waves, turbulent	账	zhàng — accounts, bill, debt, credit
粟	sù — unhusked millet, grain	谯	qiáo — tower, surname	骖	cān — two outside ones in three horse

焜	kūn — fire, flames, bright, shining	濺	jiàn — sprinkle, spray, spill, splash	漳	zhāng — name of a river in Henan
欸	ǎi — sighs, an exclamatory sound	葆	bǎo — reserve, preserve, conceal	瘩	dā — pimples
剗	chǎn — to level off, cut off, pare down, raze	恙	yàng — illness, sickness, indisposition	陞	shēng — promote, rise, ascend
榻	tà — cot, couch, bed	潞	lù — river in northern china	锤	chuí — balance weight on scale, hammer
琢	zhuó — polish jade, cut jade	簷	yán — eaves of house, brim	仆	pú — slave, servant, I
厘	lí — manage, control, 1/1000 of a foot	篷	péng — awning, covering, sail, boat	揆	kuí — prime minister, to guess, estimate
遽	jù — suddenly, unexpectedly, at once	圃	pǔ — garden, cultivated field	町	tǐng — raised path between fields
馊	sōu — spoiled, rotten, stale, rancid	潢	huáng — expanse of water, lake, pond	岖	qū — steep, sheer, rugged, rough
蟆	má — frog, toad	嚥	yàn — swallow, gulp	怂	sǒng — to alarm, to instigate, arouse, incite
琬	wǎn — the virtue of a gentleman, jade	镶	xiāng — insert, inlay, set, mount, fill	侄	zhí — nephew
庵	ān — Buddhist monastery or nunnery	瞑	míng — close eyes	赂	lù — bribe, give present
澹	dàn — calm, quiet, tranquil	杵	chǔ — pestle, baton used beat clothes	苯	běn — benzene, luxuriant
劭	shào — encourage, to excel, excellent	忡	chōng — a sad, uneasy countenance	枣	zǎo — date tree, dates, jujubes, surname
佗	tuō — other, he, surname, a load	掺	xiān — a delicate hand, mix, blend, adulterate	捅	tǒng — jab
迩	ěr — be near, be close, recently	衿	jīn — collar or lapel of garment	饕	tāo — gluttonous, greedy, covetous
皎	jiǎo — white, bright, brilliant, clear	娓	wěi — comply, complying, agreeable	镉	gé — cadmium

糯 nuò — glutinous rice, glutinous, sticky	垠 yín — boundary, bank of stream or river	潺 chán — sound of flowing water
柿 shì — persimmon	绸 chóu — silk cloth, satin damask	庠 xiáng — village school, teach
濂 lián — a waterfall, a river in Hunan	逑 qiú — collect, unite, match, pair	狈 bèi — a legendary animal with short forelegs
踝 huái — ankle	鲶 nián — sheat	傜 yáo — a minority tribe
叱 chì — scold, shout at, bawl out	缇 tí — reddish color, red, brown	懵 méng — stupid, ignorant, dull
椭 tuǒ — oval-shaped, elliptical, tubular	贻 yí — give to, hand down, bequeath	猥 wěi — vulgar, low, cheap, wanton, obscene
咁 gem4 — so (Cantonese)	粱 liáng — better varieties of millet	迭 dié — repeatedly, frequently
邰 tái — surname, state in modern Shanxi	悚 sǒng — afraid, scared, frightened	榆 yú — elm tree
脓 nóng — pus	冇 mǎo — (Cant.) have not	寨 zhài — stockade, stronghold, outpost, brothel
镁 měi — magnesium	摒 bìng — expel, cast off, arrange	徕 lái — induce, encourage to come
嗦 suō — suck	烜 xuǎn — light of the sun, to dry in the sun	萼 è — the stem and calyx of a flower, a younger brother
壬 rén — 9th heavenly stem	诧 chà — to brag, exaggerated, to wonder at	碇 dìng — anchor
镳 biāo — bit, bridle, ride	锚 máo — anchor	迥 jiǒng — distant, far, separated, different
孚 fú — brood over eggs, have confidence	陇 lǒng — mountain located between Shanxi	豺 chái — wolf, cruel, wicked, mean
悖 bèi — be contradictory to, go counter	搥 chuí — beat, pound, strike, throw, shampoo	钛 tài — titanium
肄 yì — learn, practice, study, toil	脐 qí — abdominal area of crab, navel	唢 suō — flute-like musical instrument

诙	huī — tease, joke with, ridicule, mock	拎	līng — to haul, to lift, to take	戎	róng — arms, armaments, military affair
崚	léng — hilly, steep, rugged	喳	zhā — whispering	鳕	xuě — codfish
嗣	sì — to connect, inherit, descendants, heirs	砥	dǐ — a whetstone, to polish	枋	fāng — sandalwood, tree used as timber
沽	gū — buy and sell, inferior in quality	渥	wò — moisten, soak, great, deep, dye, to enrich	黝	yǒu — black
鱿	yóu — cuttlefish	殇	shāng — die young, national mourning	蔫	yān — withered, faded, decayed, calm
爻	yáo — diagrams for divination	籁	lài — bamboo flute, pipe, various sound	孜	zī — be as diligent as possible
悥	yǒng — instigate, incite, to alarm	衙	yá — public office, official residence	痣	zhì — spots, moles, birthmark
骧	xiāng — gallop about with head uplifted	攒	zǎn — save, hoard	鎗	qiāng — rifle, small arms, hand gun
闸	zhá — sluice, flood gate, canal lock	孺	rú — child, blood relation, affection	洄	huí — a back-water, an eddy a whirlpool
昊	hào — summer time, sky, heaven	踢	táng — to fall flat, to fall on the face	沃	wò — water, irrigate, fertile, rich
妍	yán — beautiful, handsome, seductive	拽	zhuāi — drag, tow, throw, twist	牯	gǔ — cow, bull, ox
逵	kuí — thoroughfare, crossroads	泯	mǐn — destroy, eliminate, perish	龌	wò — narrow, small, dirty
銮	luán — bells hung on horse, bells hung	镛	yōng — a large bell used as a musical instrument	雉	zhì — pheasant, crenellated wall
梗	gěng — stem of flower, branch of plant	麾	huī — a pennant, flag, banner, to signal to	胤	yìn — heir, successor, progeny, posterity
馥	fù — fragrance, scent, aroma	髦	máo — flowing hair of young child	璨	càn — gems, luster of gems, lustrous
浣	wǎn — to wash, to rinse	鼐	nài — incense tripod	呗	bài — final particle of assertion pathaka

腑	fǔ — bowels, entrails, internal organs	牒	dié — documents, records, dispatch	狒	fèi — baboon
痰	tán — phlegm, mucus, spittle	剌	là — slash, cut in two, contradict	剽	piào — rob, plunder, slice off, fast
篡	cuàn — usurp	沫	mèi — to go underwater, to dive	驭	yù — drive, ride, manage, control
輦	niǎn — a hand-cart, to transport by carriage	贮	zhǔ — store, stockpile, hoard	妲	dá — concubine of last ruler of the Shang dynasty
盥	guàn — wash	莞	wǎn — smiling, a kind of aquatic herb	阖	hé — close, whole, entire, all, leaf
筏	fá — raft	炖	dùn — heat with fire, stew	纭	yún — confused, in disorder, numerous
雩	yú — offer sacrifice for rain	涧	jiàn — brook, mountain stream	筐	kuāng — bamboo basket or chest
藕	ǒu — lotus root	垓	gāi — border, boundary, frontier	垛	duǒ — heap, pile, pile up, heap up
齁	hóu — snore loudly, very, extremely	馅	xiàn — pastry filling, stuffing	芮	ruì — tiny, small, water's edge
菠	bō — spinach and similar greens	绥	suī — soothe, appease, pacify, carriage harness	躄	bì — cripple, lame
谆	zhūn — patient, earnest, earnestly	琅	láng — a variety of white carnelian, pure	汨	mì — river in Hunan province
鲑	guī — salmon, spheroides vermicularis	啜	chuò — sip, suck up, sob, weep	晤	wù — have interview with, meet
惬	qiè — be satisfied, be comfortable	苞	bāo — a variety of rush, firm, enduring, to burst forth	毗	pí — help, assist, connect, adjoin
倏	shū — hastily, suddenly, abruptly	哮	xiāo — cough, pant, roar	伎	jì — talent, skill, ability
杞	qǐ — willow, medlar tree, a small feudal state (Qi)	荃	quán — aromatic herb, fine cloth	呷	xiā — suck, swallow, drink
麹	qú — yeast, leaven, surname	糜	mí — rice gruel, congee, mashed	绯	fēi — scarlet, dark red, crimson, purpl

饯	jiàn	farewell party, see off, send off	颦	pín	frown, knit brows, with knitted	焊	huī	weld, solder
荀	xún	surname, ancient state, plant	悱	fěi	to be desirous of speaking	鸾	luán	fabulous bird
亩	mǔ	Chinese land measure, fields	龊	chuò	narrow, small, dirty	仞	rèn	ancient unit of measure (8 feet), 'fathom'
愫	sù	guileless, sincere, honest	灶	zào	furnace, kitchen range	栩	xǔ	species of oak, be glad, be pleased
浬	lǐ	nautical mile	腼	tiǎn	timid, shy, bashful	坍	tān	collapse, landslide
冽	liè	cold and raw, pure, clear	偌	ruò	thus, so, like, such	帀	fú	revolve, make circuit, turn
蒨	qiàn	lush vegetation, luxuriant growth	隋	suí	Sui dynasty, surname	劾	hé	examine into, impeach, charge
裱	biǎo	to mount maps or scrolls to paste	蜃	shèn	marine monster which can change its shape	蚌	bàng	oysters, mussels, mother-of-pearl
吆	yāo	bawl, yell, shout, cry out	毗	pí	help, assist, connect, adjoin	鳍	qí	fin
钏	chuàn	bracelet, armlet	潦	liáo	to flood, a puddle, without care	钵	bō	earthenware basin, alms bowl (Sanskrit paatra)
嗙	pǎng	boast	龈	kěn	gums	柒	qī	number seven
娼	chāng	prostitute, harlot	徛	qì	to cross over	倔	jué	stubborn, obstinate, intransigent, firm
唏	xī	weep or sob, grieve	黴	méi	mold, mildew, bacteria, fungi	碾	niàn	roller, crush, roll
瞰	kàn	watch, spy, overlook, look down	蝗	huáng	kind of locust	魇	yǎn	nightmare, bad dreams
譁	huá	noise, uproar, clamor, hubbub	钿	diàn	hairpin, gold inlaid work, filigree	悻	xìng	anger, vexation, angry, indignant
蜇	zhē	poison, sting, poisonous insect	唧	jī	chirping of insects, pump	觑	qù	peep at, watch, spy on

笊	luó — bamboo basket	窠	kē — nest, hole, indention, den	薏	yì — seed of job's tears, lotus seed
踱	duò — stroll, pace, walk slowly	腆	tiǎn — prosperous, good, protruding	睫	jié — eyelashes
謐	mì — calm, quiet, still, cautious	舫	fǎng — fancy boat, yacht	癟	piē — shrivelled up, dried up, vexed
晌	shǎng — noon, midday, moment	垛	duǒ — hardened dirt or clay, cluster	乒	pīng — used with pong for ping pong
刭	guì — amputate, cut off	娉	pīng — beautiful, attractive, charming, graceful	捻	niǎn — to twist or nip with the fingers
谟	mó — scheme, plan, plan, be without	锄	chú — hoe, eradicate	阖	gé — small side door, chamber
屹	yì — to rise high, to stand erect	哽	gěng — choke (with grief)	蜿	wān — creep, crawl
逄	páng — a surname	姗	shān — slander, ridicule, proceed slowly	獗	jué — unruly, wild, violent, lawless
帑	tǎng — a treasury, public funds	蹶	jué — stumble, fall down, trample	桧	kuài — Chinese cypress, Chinese juniper
鼾	hān — snore loudly	陲	chuí — frontier, border	窿	lóng — mine shaft, cavity, hole
箇	gè — numerary adjunct, piece, single	呆	ái — dull, dull-minded, simple, stupid	蝌	kē — tadpole
砺	lì — whetstone, sharpen	蛟	jiāo — scaly dragon with four legs	桢	zhēn — hardwood, supports, posts
匝	zā — full circle, encircle	夯	hāng — heavy load, burden, lift up	乓	pang — used with ping for ping pong
偬	zǒng — urgent	谏	jiàn — remonstrate, admonish	弭	mǐ — stop, desist, end, quell
俸	fèng — wages, salary, official emolument	烨	yè — bright, glorious, splendid, flame	弼	bì — aid, assist, help, correct
磺	huáng — sulphur, brimstone	捆	kǔn — tie up, bind, truss up, bundle	磐	pán — large rock, boulder, firm

荏	rěn beans, soft, pliable, herb	咤	zhà shout, roar, bellow, scold	崁	kǎn a place in Taiwan Tainan
泱	yāng great, expansive, agitated	洼	wā hollow, pit, depression, swamp	嵌	qiàn inlay, set in, fall into, rugged
栓	shuān wooden peg, post or stick	踵	zhǒng heel, follow, visit, call on	鞦	qiū leather stap, swing
钾	jiǎ potassium kalium	茸	róng soft, downy, buds, sprouts	弛	chí loosen, relax, unstring a bow
药	yào orris root, leaf of the iris, medicine	滢	yìng clear, pure water, lucid, glossy	玠	jiè large jade tablet used by officials at court
鹬	yù snipe, kingfisher, Tringa species (various)	钲	zhēng kind of gong used in ancient times	跻	jī ascend, go up, rise
嬷	mā mother	蚪	dǒu tadpole	鳅	qiū loach
燊	shēn luxuriant	捱	ái put off, procrastinate, endure	狩	shòu winter hunting, imperial tour
骼	gé bone, skeleton, corpse	掬	jú to grasp or hold with both hands	酝	yùn liquor, spirits, wine, ferment
祀	sì to sacrifice, worship	琛	chēn treasure, valuables	獭	tà otter
箝	qián tweezers, pliers, tongs, pincers	菡	hàn buds, lotus buds	隹	zhuī bird, KangXi radical 172
邝	kuàng surname	楔	xiè wedge, gatepost, foreword	缱	qiǎn attached to, inseparable, entangled
诒	yí bequeath, pass on to future generations	婶	shěn wife of father's younger brother	擘	bò thumb, break, tear open, rip
愠	yùn angry, indignant, resentful	采	biàn distinguish, KangXi radical 165	稔	rěn ripe grain, harvest, to know, be familiar with
槭	cù maple	帷	wéi tent, curtain, screen	黉	héng school
镰	lián sickle	鼴	yǎn a kind of insectivorous rodent	芎	qiōng a kind of herb

埤 **pí** — add, increase, attach, low fence	邢 **xíng** — surname, state in today's Hebei	呓 **yì** — talk in one's sleep, somniloquy
缥 **piǎo** — light blue silk, dim, misty	骛 **wù** — gallop, rush about, pursue, run	铀 **yóu** — uranium
偃 **yǎn** — cease, lay off, lay down	闾 **lǘ** — village of twenty-five families	恫 **tōng** — in pain, sorrowful
瞿 **qū** — surname	蟒 **mǎng** — python, boa constrictor	淦 **gàn** — river in Jiangxi province
湮 **yīn** — bury, sink, block up, stain	涤 **dí** — wash, cleanse, purify, sweep	琥 **hǔ** — jewel in shape of tiger, amber
轧 **yà** — crush by weight, grind	槙 **diān** — a twig, an ornamental evergreen	忝 **tiǎn** — disgraced, ashamed, self-deprecating
崧 **sōng** — high mountain, lofty, eminent	诌 **zōu** — play with words, quip, talk nonse	飒 **sà** — the sound of the wind, bleak, melancholy
喋 **dié** — nag, chatter, babble, twitter	舶 **bó** — large, ocean-going vessel	箕 **jī** — sieve, dust pan, garbage bag
墩 **dūn** — heap, mound, block of stone	哒 **dā** — sound made to get a horse to move forward	晾 **liàng** — air-dry, sun-dry
砷 **shēn** — arsenic	濡 **rú** — immerse, moisten, wet, damp	猾 **huá** — crafty, cunning, shrewd, deceitful
阂 **hé** — blocked or separated, to prevent	鞯 **qiān** — swing	宦 **huàn** — officialdom, government official
檄 **sù** — shrub	鲷 **diāo** — pagrosomus major, porgy	佞 **nìng** — flattery, glib
叟 **sǒu** — old man, elder	团 **tuán** — sphere, ball, circle, mass, lump	沅 **yuán** — name of a river in western Hunan
疡 **yáng** — ulcers, sores, infection	啬 **sè** — miserly, thrifty, stingy, stopped up, constipated	眈 **dān** — gloat, stare at, to delay, to loiter, to hinder
肴 **yáo** — prepared meat, food	豨 **xī** — pig, hog	囤 **dùn** — grain basket, bin for grain
裆 **dāng** — crotch or seat of pants, pants	蕨 **jué** — pteris aquilina, common bracken	胱 **guāng** — bladder

慉	bì — obstinate, stubborn, headstrong	稼	jià — sow grain, sheaves of grain	嵋	méi — Omei mountain in Sichuan
瑙	nǎo — agate, cornelian	稷	jì — god of cereals, minister of agriculture	忖	cǔn — guess, suppose, conjecture
荟	huì — luxuriant, flourishing, abundant	妩	wǔ — charming, enchanting	嚏	tì — sneeze
箴	zhēn — needle, probe, admon	绻	quǎn — affectionate, solicitous	湍	tuān — rapid water current, rapids
爰	yuán — lead on to, therefore, then	颔	hàn — chin, jowl, give nod	痧	shā — cholera, colic
戕	qiāng — kill, slay, wound, injure, hurt	绢	juàn — kind of thick stiff silk	嗝	gé — cackling of fowls to gag, to vomit
褓	bǎo — swaddling cloth, infancy	梆	bāng — watchman's rattle	晞	xī — dry, expose sun, dawn
锢	gù — run metal into cracks, confine	剁	duò — chop by pounding, mince, hash	慑	shè — afraid, scared, fearful
嗟	jiē — sigh, alas	泷	lóng — raining, wet, soaked, a river in Guangdong	诤	zhēng — to expostulate, to remonstrate
暝	míng — dark, obscure	帼	guó — women's headgear, mourning cap	牴	dǐ — gore, butt, resist
琏	lián — a vessel used hold grain offerings	昴	mǎo — one of the 28 constellations	诩	xǔ — boast, brag, popular, well known, to flatter
篆	zhuàn — seal script, seal, official stamp	攫	jué — snatch away, seize, catch with	甯	níng — peaceful
睨	nì — look askance at, glare at, squint	缎	duàn — satin	蹬	dèng — step on, tread on, lose energy
犁	lí — plow	蛆	qū — maggots	诋	dǐ — slander, condemn, reproach
缨	yīng — a chin strap, tassel, to annoy, bother	睾	gāo — testicle	婢	bì — servant girl, your servant
倘	tǎng — if	霁	jì — to clear up after rain, to cease be angry	琅	láng — a variety of white carnelian, pure

熏	xūn smoke, fog, vapor, smoke, cure	啻	chì only, merely, just like, stop at	捎	shāo to select, to take, to carry
皿	mǐn shallow container, rad. no. 108	暄	xuān warm, comfortable, warm, genial	躅	zhú walk carefully, hesitate, falter
吃	chī eat, drink, suffer, endure, bear	宥	yòu forgive, pardon, indulge	埕	chéng a large, pear-shaped earthenware jar
涣	huàn scatter, scattered, dispersed	怦	pēng eager, ardent, impulsive, anxious	傧	bìn entertain guests
鲥	shí reeves' shad, hilsa herring	迸	bèng gush out, burst forth, split	釜	fǔ cauldron, pot, kettle
踯	zhí waver, hesitate, be irresolute	簑	suō a coat raincoat	僮	tóng page, boy servant
兹	zī now, here, this, time, year	衲	nà mend, sew, patch, line, quilt	杳	yǎo obscure, dark, mysterious, deep
姒	sì wife of elder brother	嬿	yàn lovely	忪	zhōng quiet, calm, tranquil, peaceful
鲲	kūn spawn, roe, fy	槁	gǎo wither, withered, rotten, dead	馋	chán gluttonous, greedy, lewd, lecherous
牲	shēng abundant, numerous, crowd	癞	lài leprosy, scabies, mange, shoddy	咋	zhà question-forming particle, why? how? what?
翌	yì bright, daybreak, dawn, the next day	栱	gǒng large peg, stake, post, pillar	唠	láo chat, jaw, gossip, talk
轶	yì rush forth, surpass, excel	驮	tuó carry on back	铬	gè chromium
驽	nú tired, old horse, old, weak	阜	fù mound, abundant, ample, numerous	啐	cuì to taste, to sip, to spit
猷	yóu plan, scheme, plan, plot, way	癈	fèi abrogate, terminate, discard	蝨	shī louse, bed bug
楹	yíng column, pillar, numerary adjunct	氨	ān ammonia, hydrogen nitride	菅	jiān coarse grass, themedia forskali
泞	nìng mud, miry, muddy, stagnant	戟	jǐ halberd with crescent blade	拮	jié laboring hard, occupied, pursue

踞	jù	crouch, squat, sit, occupy	忐	tǎn	timorous, nervous	骅	huá	an excellent horse
彧	yù	refined, cultured, polished	纰	pí	spoiled silk, hem of dress, mista	坛	tán	an earthenware jar, a jug
鄀	yǐng	state in today's Hubei province	聒	guā	clamor, din, hubbub	蹒	shān	stagger, limp
犛	lí	a black ox, a yak	驷	sì	team of four horses	姣	jiāo	beautiful, handsome, pretty
谪	zhé	charge, blame, disgrace, demote, punish	忑	tè	fearful, nervous, timid	焊	hàn	weld, solder
饷	xiǎng	rations and pay for soldiers	钠	nà	sodium, natrium, sharpen wood	娄	lóu	surname, a constellation, to wear
倭	wēi	dwarf, dwarfish, short	胭	yān	rouge, cosmetics	邋	lá	rags
秧	yāng	rice seedlings, young rice plants	恻	cè	feel anguish, feel compassion	宸	chén	imperial, imperial palace
鲈	lú	sea perch, sea bass	妤	yú	beautiful, fair, handsome	椿	chūn	father, a plant with white flowers
锂	lǐ	lithium	猬	wèi	hedgehog	嶙	lín	precipitous
醺	xūn	get drunk, be intoxicated	嘈	cáo	noisy	逖	tì	far, distant, keep at distance
涘	sì	river bank, water's edge	爿	qiáng	half of tree trunk	鮀	tuó	snakefish
滕	téng	an ancient state in Shandong province	荪	sūn	aromatic grass, iris, flower	殡	bìn	encoffin, embalm, funeral
嫦	cháng	name of a moon goddess	臧	zāng	good, right, generous, command	峋	xún	ranges of hills stretching on beyond another peaks
坻	chí	an islet, a rock in a river, an embankment	暾	tūn	morning sun, sunrise	阋	xì	feud, fight, quarrel
钘	xíng	ancient wine vessel	俎	zǔ	chopping board or block, painted	据	jù	to occupy, take possession of, a base

蜒	yán millipede	褉	xiē short garments	邑	yì area, district, city, state
缈	miǎo indistinct, dim, minute, distant	涎	xián saliva	沚	zhǐ islet in stream, small sandbar
沪	hù Shanghai, river near Shanghai	綵	cǎi varicolored silk, variegated	轫	rèn a block that keeps a wheel from moving
捺	nà to press down heavily with the fingers	拴	shuān bind with rope, fasten	耆	qí man of sixty, aged, old
柑	gān tangerine, loose-skinned orange	颍	yǐng river in Anhui	浚	jùn dredge
喟	kuì heave sigh, sigh	棣	dì kerria japonica plant, cherry	嗷	áo loud clamor, sound of wailing
熨	yùn iron, press	挓	zhā to open out, to expand	甕	wèng earthen jar, jar for ashes
槐	huái locust tree	娩	miǎn give birth child, complaisant	镴	là solder, tin
蕤	ruí drooping leaves, fringe soft, delicate	腋	yì armpit	瘁	cuì feel tired, be weary, be worn out
铿	kēng strike, beat, stroke, jingling	澍	shù timely rain, life-giving rain	莠	yǒu weeds, tares, undesirable, evil
糸	mì silk, KangXi radical 120	悌	tì brotherly, respectful	勺	sháo spoon, ladle, unit of volume
涌	yǒng surge up, bubble up, gush forth	枰	píng smooth board, chessboard, chess	伝	chuán summon, propagate, transmit
锌	xīn zincum	饴	yí sweet-meats, sweet-cakes, syrup	幡	fān pennant, banner, streamer, flag
铄	shuò melt, smelt, shine	胯	kuà pelvis, groin, thighs	岌	jí perilous, hazardous, high, steep
痢	lì dysentery	姝	shū a beautiful girl	诳	kuáng deceive, lie, delude, cheat
醃	yān marinate, pickle, salt	瞠	chēng look at, stare at, gaze at	晡	bū late afternoon

獠	liáo	to hunt at night by torches	膫	liáo	the fat covering the intestines, the omentum	腮	sāi	lower part of face, jaw, gills of a fish
榛	zhēn	hazelnut, thicket, underbrush	烯	xī	alkene	膊	bó	shoulders, upper arms
淅	xī	water used wash rice, to wash ric	纣	zhòu	name of an emperor, saddle part	佶	jí	strong, robust, exact, correct
葩	pā	flowers	嫡	dí	legal wife, child of legal wife	狞	níng	ferocious appearance, hideous
缄	jiān	seal, close, bind, letter	诿	wěi	pass buck, lay blame on others	帛	bó	silks, fabrics, wealth, property
甬	yǒng	path, river in Ningbo, Ningbo	芩	qín	salt marsh plant	玑	jī	pearl that is not quite round
鹫	jiù	condor, vulture	豊	lǐ	abundant, lush, bountiful, plenty	倜	tì	raise high, unrestrained
蹴	cù	kick, tread on, leap, solemn	镂	lòu	carve, inlay, engrave, tattoo	丘	qiū	hill, elder, empty, a name
腓	féi	calf, avoid, be ill, wither	邸	dǐ	official residence, residence of	脯	fǔ	dried meat, preserved fruits
毁	huǐ	destroy, ruin, injure, slander	菀	wǎn	luxuriance of growth	犊	dú	calf, victim of sacrifice
珂	kē	inferior kind of jade	盅	zhōng	small cup or bowl	挹	yì	to bale out, to decant liquids
烩	huì	ragout, cook, braise	锜	qí	a kind of pen, a kind of chisel	胳	gē	armpit, arms
叼	diāo	holding in mouth	馄	hún	dumpling soup, wonton	猝	cù	abruptly, suddenly, abrupt
谀	yú	flatter, truckle	卞	biàn	to be impatient, in a hurry, excitable	俦	chóu	companion, mate, colleague
雎	jū	osprey, fishhawk, hold back	堇	jǐn	celery, aconite	炘	xīn	brilliant, shining, bright
鹄	hú	target	酮	tóng	ketones	氟	fú	fluorine

桀	jié	chicken roost, ancient emperor	帚	zhǒu	broom, broomstick	荔	lì	lichee
洱	ěr	a lake in Yunnan	窖	jiào	pit, cellar	薮	sǒu	marsh, swamp, wild country
捂	wǔ	resist	锾	huán	measure, money, coins	夤	yín	distant place, remote, deep
璐	lù	beautiful variety of jade	恚	huì	anger, rage	氦	hài	fluorine
颚	è	jaw	遢	tà	careless, negligent, slipshod	渤	bó	swelling, name of a sea gulf
舀	yǎo	dip, ladle, ladle	猕	mí	macacus monkey	碉	diāo	room made of stone, watchtower
矬	cuó	a dwarf	氰	qīng	cyanogen, ethane dinitrile	韭	jiǔ	scallion, leek, radical 179
帘	lián	a blind, screen, curtain	谒	yè	visit, pay respects to	噤	jìn	close, be silent, be unable speak
蓑	suō	rain coat made of straw, coir, etc.	蹼	pú	webbed feet of waterfowl	棹	zhuō	oar, boat
拧	níng	pinch, twist, wring, determined	臾	yú	moment, instant, short while	疝	shàn	hernia, rupture
蛭	zhì	leech	烊	yáng	to smelt, to melt	绁	xiè	bridle, halter
只	qí	only, merely, but	邈	miǎo	far, distant, remote, slight	踽	jǔ	to walk alone, self-reliant
尻	kāo	end of spine, buttocks, sacrum	淙	cóng	gurgling sound of water	嘹	liáo	used describe clarity of voice, resonant
夆	fēng	resist	涪	fú	river in Sichuan province	肓	huāng	region between heart and diaphragm
刮	guā	to blow	庖	páo	kitchen, cooking, cuisine	鸢	yuān	kite, Milvus species (various)
炤	zhào	illumine, light up, reflect	跺	duò	stamp feet, step	愍	mǐn	pity, sympathize with

讴	ōu — to sing, songs	壑	hè — bed of torrent, narrow ravine	辘	lù — windlass, pulley, capstan, wheel
胛	jiǎ — the shoulder, shoulder blade	绛	jiàng — deep red, river in Shanxi provinc	匾	biǎn — flat, round split-bamboo contain
臊	sāo — rank, rancid, frowzy, fetid, bashful	壅	yōng — to obstruct	睇	dì — look at, glance at, stare at
忉	dāo — grieved, distressed in mind	刈	yì — cut off, reap, mow, sickle	蹙	cù — urgent, suddenly, grieve, lament
泵	bèng — pump	珣	xún — name of a kind of jade	孃	niáng — troubled, oppressed, fat, mother
畦	qí — sections in vegetable farm	蠋	zhú — caterpillar	戍	shù — defend borders, guard frontiers
蝎	hé — scorpion	羡	xiàn — envy, admire, praise, covet	靳	jìn — strap on a horse's breast
殁	mò — die, death, dead	伕	fū — common laborer	蹒	mán — to jump over, to limp
佚	yì — indulge in pleasures, flee	囱	cōng — chimney, funnel	嘤	yīng — seek friends, also used in names
趺	fū — sit cross-legged, back of the foo	脩	xiū — dried meat	砾	lì — gravel, pebbles, potsherds
臬	niè — law, rule, door post	罄	qìng — exhaust, run out, use up, empty	艋	měng — small boat
邬	wū — various place names, surname	掣	chè — drag, pull, hinder by pulling back	钨	wù — tungsten, wolfram
缭	liáo — wind round, rap around, bind	糟	zāo — sediment, dregs, pickle	撬	qiào — lift, raise, pry open
噪	zào — be noisy, chirp loudly	孿	mǎn — to see, witness, inspect	哆	chǐ — tremble, shiver, shudder, quiver
脍	kuài — minced meat or fish	孑	jié — remaining, left-over, lonely	氐	dǐ — name of an ancient tribe
嘎	á — hoarse of voice	痉	jìng — convulsions, fits	赣	gàn — Jiangxi province, places therein

揩	kāi	rub and wipe, dust, clean	芊	qiān	exuberant and vigorous foliage	咱	zǎn	a dual pronoun, I, you and me, we two
蹑	niè	tread, step on, follow, track	鼬	yòu	weasel, mustela itatis	甥	shēng	sister's child
拄	zhǔ	lean on, post, prod, ridicule	荧	yíng	shine, shimmer, shining, dazzling	狰	zhēng	fierce-looking, ferocious
鲛	jiǎo	shark	跶	tà	stumble, slip	陛	bì	steps leading throne, throne
诎	qù	bend, stoop, crouch, to yield	苹	pín	apple	鞑	dá	tartars
愔	yīn	comfortable, contented, peaceful	捩	liè	twist with hands, snap, tear	凌	líng	pass over, cross, traverse
顸	hān	large face, flat face, stupid	桎	zhí	fetters, shackles, handcuffs	刎	wěn	behead, cut throat
榭	xiè	kiosk, pavilion	蠕	ruǎn	eumenes polifomis, kind of wasp	埂	gěng	ditches for irrigation, hole
罡	gāng	the name of a certain stars	颢	hào	luminous, white, hoary	圜	yuán	circle, surround, encircle
赁	rèn	rent, hire, hired person	纔	cái	talent, ability, just, only	刨	bào	carpenter's plane, plane, level
筊	jiǎo	bamboo rope, bamboo object used	彊	qiáng	stubborn, uncompromising	筌	quán	bamboo fish trap
莋	zuò	mat	蹊	xī	footpath, trail, track	壸	kǔn	palace corridor or passageway
谖	xuān	forget, lie, cheat, deceive	胫	jìng	shinbone, calf of leg	宕	dàng	stone quarry, cave dwelling
珪	guī	a jade table conferred upon feudal princes	揶	yé	make fun of, ridicule	蓼	liǎo	smartweed, polygonum
赀	zī	property, wealth, to count	屄	bī	the vagina	觎	yú	desire strongly, covet, long for
鹧	zhè	partridge	雕	diāo	engrave, inlay, carve, exhaust	掴	guó	box one's ears, slap

膡	shèng	leftovers, residue, remains	扈	hù	escort, retinue, insolent	淬	cuì	temper, dye, soak, change, alter
赟	bì	forge ahead, energetic, surname	蝣	yóu	mayfly, emphemera strigata	綑	kǔn	coil, roll, bundle, tie up
潸	shān	weep, tears flowing	瘐	yǔ	to die in prison from cold and hunger	玎	dīng	jingling, tinkling
辍	chuò	stop, suspend, halt	赈	zhèn	relieve, aid distressed, rich	鸲	qú	mynah, Erithacus species (various)
嘀	dí	backbite	昃	zè	afternoon, the sun in the afternoon sky	婬	yín	obscene, licentious, lewd
囿	yòu	pen up, limit, constrain	坳	ào	a hollow in the ground, a cavity, depression	滮	biāo	flow, (Cant.) to ooze, to spurt
蓡	sēn	ginseng, huge	饨	tún	stuffed dumplings	雹	báo	hail
畀	bì	to give	渭	wèi	name of a river in Shanxi	掔	qiān	sturdy
胝	zhī	callous, corn	搾	zhà	to crush with the hand, press, squeeze, extract	觊	jì	covet, long for, desire
崽	zǎi	a child, a servant, a diminutive	沓	tà	connected, joined, repeated	褛	lǚ	lapel, collar, tattered, threadbare
衮	gǔn	ceremonial dress worn by the emperor	儺	nuó	rich	嗲	dia3	(Cant.) saliva, intensifying particle
柰	nài	crab-apple tree, endure, bear	鏖	áo	to fight to the end, engage in a fierce battle	嵬	wēi	high, lofty, precipitous
濠	háo	moat, trench, ditch	鹜	mù	duck	忒	tè	too, very-usually of objectionable things
揄	yú	lift, raise, praise, hang, flap	挛	lván	tangled, entwined, crooked	缰	jiāng	reins, halter, bridle
锉	cuò	carpenter's file, file smooth	筵	yán	bamboo mat, feast, banquet	鹄	gū	species of Taiwan pigeon
糠	kāng	chaff, bran, husks, poor	礴	bó	fill, extend	亳	bó	name of district in Anhui, capital of Yin

幔	màn — curtain, screen, tent	宓	mì — quiet, silent, in good health	瓒	zàn — ceremonial libation cup
陕	shǎn — mountain pass, Shaanxi province	腱	jiàn — tendons	忾	kài — anger, wrath, hatred, enmity
鳌	áo — huge sea turtle	玷	diàn — flaw in gem, flaw in character	谗	chán — slander, defame, misrepresent
鬟	huán — dress hair in coiled knot, maid	栲	kǎo — mangrove	篓	lǒu — bamboo basket
旌	jīng — banner or flag adorned with feathers, to signal	幄	wò — tent, mosquito net	翳	yì — shade, screen, to hide, screen
棻	fén — kind of wood from which perfume	荞	qiáo — buckwheat	靛	diàn — indigo, any blue dye
铛	dāng — frying pan, warming vessel	啥	hān — a sound, to put in the mouth	轭	è — yoke, collar, to restrain
壕	háo — trench, ditch, channel, moat	褡	dá — inner shirt or singlet	羌	qiāng — Qiang nationality, surname
撂	lvè — put down, put aside, drop	犷	guǎng — fierce, rude, uncivilized	讫	qì — finish, conclude, stop, exhaust
洵	xún — true, real, truly, really	锭	dìng — spindle, slab, cake, tablet	髻	jì — hair rolled up in a bun, topknot
齰	cuò — to bite	胼	pián — callus, calluses	榔	láng — palm
砝	fá — balance weights	涔	cén — river in Shaanxi, murky torrent	仃	dīng — lonely, solitary
黔	qián — black, Guizhou	涸	hé — dried up, exhausted, tired, dry	婀	ē — be beautiful, be graceful
搀	chān — to give a helping hand, to support, hold up	梏	gù — handcuffs, manacles, fetters	蛔	huí — tapeworm
纂	zuǎn — edit, compile, topknot, chignon	堀	kū — cave, hole	倬	zhuō — noticeable, large, clear, distinct
晟	chéng — clear, bright, splendor, brightness	纮	hóng — string, vast, expansive	镧	láng — lock lanthanum

琱 diāo — engrave, inlay, carve, exhaust	凊 qìng — surname	寤 wù — few, scarce, empty, deserted
鮪 wěi — kind of sturgeon, tuna	囥 kàng — hide	珞 luò — kind of necklace
蚜 yá — plant louse, aphids	登 dēng — ceremonial vessel	搵 wèn — to search, look for
倨 jù — arrogant, haughty, rude	戡 kān — subjugate, subdue, quell, kill	迤 yǐ — wind, walk out of straight path
埼 qí — headland	臏 bìn — the kneecap	儆 jǐng — warn, warning
擤 xǐng — to blow the nose with fingers	纨 wán — white silk, fine silk, gauze	忻 xīn — delightful, joyful, pleasant
蠔 háo — oyster	熇 hè — bake	囍 xǐ — double happiness
瓯 ōu — bowl, cup, small tray	祚 zuò — throne, bless, blessing, happiness	蜉 fú — mayfly, kind of large insect
骈 pián — team of horses, associate, join	懟 duì — hate, abhor, hatred, resentment	褊 biǎn — cramped, narrow, crowded, mean
镑 bàng — pound sterling	熏 xūn — smoke, fog, vapor, smoke, cure	俚 lǐ — rustic, vulgar, unpolished, mean
恪 kè — respectful, reverent	觔 jīn — catty	踫 pèng — collide, bump into
弁 biàn — conical cap worn during Zhou dynasty	啣 xián — hold in mouth, harbor, cherish	锟 kūn — ancient treasured sword
芍 shuò — peony, water chestnuts	荨 xún — nettle	擢 zhuó — pull up, draw up, select
盹 dùn — to doze, to nap, to nod	旸 yáng — rising sun, sunshine	斡 wò — revolve, rotate, turn
痍 yí — wound, bruise, sore	忸 niǔ — blush, be bashful, be ashamed	轵 zhì — low rear portion of cart
0 0 — 0	0 0 — 0	0 0 — 0